ONE SUMMER MORNING IN MY GARDEN

by

Della Livorno

All rights reserved

No part of this publication may be reproduced, stored in or introduced into a retrieval system or transmitted in any form, or by any means (electronic, mechanical, photocopying, recording or otherwise) without the prior written permission of the publisher.

Apart from any fair dealing for the purpose of private study, research, criticism or review, this bool can be utilized only if appropriately referenced under the Copywrite, Designs and Patents Act, 1988.

All sketches and paintings have been executed by the author using different media, namely watercolours, coloured pencils, ink, charcoal, pencil and natural botanical dyes.

© 2024 Della Livorno

ISBN: 978-1-4461-4026-0

'If you have a garden
and a library,
you have everything
you need'

Cicero 46 BC

INTRODUCTION

I have always thought of a private garden as the extension of my soul, and have been longing to possess one all my life. The time came while living in England when two of our houses had a beautiful garden attached, but my work commitments were such I could hardly enjoy the luxury of free time spent on their luscious green lawns.

Then, back in Italy, by a twist of serendipity I finally struck lucky and was able to acquire an amazingly serene piece of land bound by ancient dry-stone walls. However, not only did I come by a green plot but I also made a long term friendship with the people who sold it to me.

I have certainly embraced my new environment full of promise, suffusing my soul with positive thoughts. Indeed my garden has become the mirror image of my soul and, because I spend a great deal of time in it, I realize I am living in accordance with one of Marcus Aurelius's most renowned of quotes:

'Your days are numbered. Use them to throw open the windows of your soul to the sun. If you do not, the sun will soon set, and you with it.'

The strong attraction I felt on the two occasions I happened to walk past the little plot gate, was nothing less than the Spirit of the Place calling upon my wish to embrace the garden-to-be proper and match my passion with the love that previous owners proffered on it.

The Spirit of the Place, or Genius Loci, cogitated benevolently behind the scenes to bring us all together for the well-being of the place itself. Nine months into my project of transforming a barren, neglected square into an English-style, green paradise, I was inspired by the incredible circumstances which led me to be in my present position, to write my story as I lived it with my heart bursting with gratitude towards the people who, by depriving themselves of their original plot, acquired both a transformed garden and my friendship.

The sensation of elation I feel while inside my garden can only be rendered as lively and upbeat as I experience it by narrating it in a *stream of consciousness*. Nothing in a garden is logical, sequential or predictable and Nature does not work in a systematic fashion. The colours, scents, sounds, shapes and textures all hit the senses at once besides the daily surprises of, for instance, a gastropod sliming over the grass kissed by the fat rain drops; or a flower which has burst open with the most captivating of hues that only a few hours before was still constrained inside its sepals; or a shower of white petals falling from the pear trees when a sudden gust of wind whips up a vortex in the air.

All the afore mentioned events and more may happen at once all together only to subside and disappear as soon as they have materialized, to be replaced soon afterwards by other even more enthralling phenomena such as the sudden soil eruption out of a mole's tunnel or the loud thumping noise of the neighbour's cat jumping from the lower branches of the plum tree onto the top of my stone-wall to disappear as swiftly as he came by plunging into the public footpath below.

There is no other way to convey all the feelings, sightings, experiences and memories I have packed in a few months than to tell them in a stream of thoughts which bubbled up inside my mind over the three hours that one summer morning I spent in my garden while waiting for my newly acquired friends to visit me and discover what their former land looked in the present.

Words are essential to describe both events and accompanying sensations but we all know that a picture is worth a thousands words, as the old adage goes. As far as I am concerned words allow the readers to create their own mental images which can by far be more powerful and compelling than a printed static picture on the page. To be in keeping with my literary technique of expressing my thoughts as they surfaced to my mind I, nevertheless, created drawings and watercolours relative to my narrative and just as in a '*stream of thoughts*', they are portrayed to represent a '*stream of pictures*'. As a matter of fact the human mind would not naturally describe a walled garden in an orderly manner by following the perimeter of the walls inch by inch, but when called upon the memory of a given garden, haphazard images would start to take shape superimposed in space and time as our subconscious mind chooses to recall them. That is the beauty of our irrational intellect, our creativity when let free to roam and to enjoy what comes into it in a continuous manner like the water in a stream in constant movement, ebbing and flowing, forming ripples and whirlpools, encircling any obstacle along its path, but never stopping.

The highly organic nature of my garden led me to choose a name that reminds me of the love and respect that a similar land back in my acquired country, as a British citizen, always inspired me and demanded much admiration: 'Highgrove Garden'. The chosen name for my little land thus became 'Little HighGrove garden'.

This book is a testament of the friendship between two families who have the happiness of a little plot of land at their heart and who were unbeknownst of the Spirit of the Place's kind machinations to bring them together inside its magical, natural realm, our garden.

PREFACE

After acquiring a little plot of land surrounded by dry-stone walls, the author reminisces the experiences and sensations of the past nine months spent to transform the barren green space into an English garden paradise. Her memories and immediate observations bubble up in her mind over the three hours she spends sitting in her garden one summer morning while waiting for her new friends, the former owners of the plot, to turn up for their very first visit.

The garden layout is meant to be a surprise for them because they last saw their land the year earlier, before they sold it to the author. The encounter of the former owners with the new proprietor, the writer, leads the latter to finally discover the reasons behind the sale. The motives are a real eye opener and truly astounding and they point to one and only one entity, the Spirit of the Place, otherwise known as Genius Loci, who plotted lovingly behind the scenes to lure its guests all together in order to ensure its potential to flourish and to be cherished.

The author is keen on stressing out that she does not feel she owns the garden but she is the Genius Loci's guest of honour who inhabits the garden and welcomed her in its realm with open fronds. Therefore, the author's principal duty is to protect the garden along with all the living creatures it supports in order to prevent it from coming to any harm. As a matter of fact the Genius Loci is the garden itself, and both the garden and the author have assured their true happiness by allowing their reciprocal hearts to smile within their shared wonderland.

The peaceful, calm and all encompassing atmosphere within the stone-walls of this magical garden represent a miracle which was only possible through the selfless and generous heart of the previous owner, Maria Carlone who, at the age of 90 years old, retains the beauty and gaiety of a young woman whose life philosophy is to share and to love.

DEDICATION

I dedicate this book to Maria Carlone, my benefactress, previous owner of my Little HighGrove Garden, whose generosity and kindness has etched a huge smile on my heart for eternity, and has gifted me with the most precious of human sentiments, her friendship.

What a splendid summer morning!

I am waiting to welcome my benefactors into my well-guarded hideaway. They have come back to their holiday abode to spend some time amongst the villagers and to enjoy the privacy of a plunge into the cool, transparent waters of the local mountain stream.

I experience the same nervous expectancy of their opinion now, as I did then, when one late August morning, exactly one year ago, we met under fateful, auspicious circumstances and, unknowingly, we became privy to a shared dream.

"So, are you interested in the purchase, and how much would you hope to get it for?"

It was clear that within ten minutes of meeting one another, negotiations were well under way, leading me to confidently say that the object of my desire was within my grasp.

"I do not know, I have never bought anything similar, therefore, I'd rather leave the final decision to you".

"We can meet half way", I was told, "nothing is impossible; what really matters in life is true friendship, I rely on my faith in the Holy Black Madonna, and pray. OK, let's exchange telephone numbers because in one week's time we'll be gone and we'll contact our surveyor for establishing a lawful, reasonable asking price. We shall be in touch presently".

What stroke of luck, what pleasant, well-meaning people, I pondered as I left their premises. Whatever the charge, I must have it; I'll get a loan from the bank if necessary and will somehow repay the debt, I promised myself, because deep inside I knew what happened that day was once in a lifetime's opportunity which if missed, would not repeat itself.

My initial exultation shifted into a state of intolerable anxiety and then back into excitement again, and so back and forth, as the days, the weeks and eventually one and a half months went by with no news from my potential sellers. No answers to appease my qualms.

What will they make of the utter transformation I diligently carried out with knowledge (acquired over the past year, with a view to coming by a miracle), passion, drive and back-breaking physical toil? Will they match the outcome with my initial project made of written goals, sketches and visually impacting watercolours? Will they perceive a sense of magic, surreal and utter uniqueness as I do?

One evening the phone rang, its tone accompanied by the name of the caller on the display. My heart missed a beat, I hesitated a few seconds to ensure it really was whom I thought it might be, then, a brief, cordial exchange left me in tears, literally dumbfounded. The surveyor suggested an asking price of nine hundred Euros which my benefactor, Maria, was willing to reduce to eight hundred Euros. Would I accept the offer, she inquisitively asked on the line. My prompt reply was loud and clear:

"Yes!" accompanied by a heartfelt, "Thank you!" for her outright generosity.

The two of us were happy a swift agreement had been reached and the proceedings for the formal sale could be commenced and hopefully brought to an expeditious conclusion within a few weeks.

I now look around me with affection or better still sheer love of Nature; what I can feel, smell, hear and write about is priceless, yet its cost in monetary terms was ludicrous. I had braced myself for at least five thousand Euros and yet what I had to pay in comparison with my estimate, was inconsequent. My benefactors will be here soon for the first time in one year; I shall never fathom what made them part with what is now my precious gift other than selfless understanding of my then existential predicament? Not only am I the beneficiary of a new lease of life but also of a freshly acquired friendship which I cherish with equal ardour. Generosity is a rare attribute in people these days; the thinking goes there is no point in promoting someone else's happiness without any personal gain. Yet, these people did lose out both in terms of their finances with little gain on their part, and of something that used to belong to them which is now carrying a moral promise of a budding closeness amongst all the parties involved. I welcome this unexpected ray of bright sunshine into my life after the prolonged endurance of so much pain and disappointment that the later years of my nursing career brought into my life.

The sun is peeping out through a thick layer of graded black and grey clouds which are slowly building up above the mountains; a sign of some orographic storm approaching? The lack of wind does not incline me to believe that any precipitation is due any time soon, therefore, my surprise will not be spoilt. The sun is hot in the height of summer, but some recent heavy storms have lowered the temperature by several degrees thus making our presence outdoor more bearable. Today, however, my guests of honour have been invited in the middle of the morning when some night's dew is still be-jewelling with winking glitters the emerald grass blades, like a sequined green counterpane spread on the ground. Yes, after almost five interminable years of my leaving England, the house refurbishment, the pandemic and a mostly painful and fruitless search for what I missed the most in my life, yes, I can say with a quiver in my voice:

"I have a garden again!"

A real dry-stone walled garden, one kilometre away from home as the crow flies, and a stone throw away from the village main road where, at the end of our narrow, cobbled alleyway, is a beautiful, all-day-long-drumming fountain which collects inside a large syenite vat before joining the subterranean drains. What I can enjoy now is definitely a far cry from the day my husband and I reached the Bed and Breakfast and unloaded our suitcases from the taxi, when I was acutely aware of having eyed every single plot of ground be it a front yard or a proper green cultivated area, while being driven. My envy quickly turned into anger and spite even for what I no longer owned. This melee of negative feelings, this psychological upheaval reached a climax of misery which eventually became channeled into an obsession, and translated into a frantic search for a piece of paradise to call my own. If my garden had to be sold with the house because the mortgage was still outstanding, then as a matter of fact, what I used to call 'mine', legally no longer belonged to me. That's the reason why, subconsciously, I knew to never design that garden, to never add any feature and to limit myself to planting a few trees, a couple of shrubs and only committed to keeping it tidy, although often with a bolding and patchy lawn. Yet, I loved it. I savoured the potential it held should I, one day, by a curious twist of fate, manage to repay my mortgage in full and, under different circumstances, have stayed in England. But, it was not to be, thus, I must be grateful for my Italian house and the verdant countryside and nearby mountains that are free to roam, I assured myself. Yes, it is nice to entertain an idea but it is unfortunate that in fact I lulled myself into a false sense of security, because reality in my picture-perfect scenery dwelled in the past. The present was far from pleasant and I found out one autumn afternoon when, after settling the house renovation project with the builder, I decided to take a long walk into the Nature paradise that was now to be a second-best substitute for my beloved English garden I'd recently lost. The hamlet on the hill had not changed, only its inhabitants had; some were new, many were dead (retrospectively, no big loss!), few just renting during the tourist season. Passed the village, the meadow falling towards the stream looked diminished in size with derelict metal fencing around what there used to be plentiful, single allotments; how many were there, six, seven, I cannot precisely recall; and the people who owned them, obsessive, selfish and at times suitably aggressive individuals who did not either understand or approve of my need to hide deep in the heart of the forest beyond the stream, to study and to write in the open air. Now they were gone, so I was free at last to move as I pleased away from the gaze of nightmarish, preying eyes. I would relive the joy and love of Nature that accompanied my youth, the breeze, the tender hues of the trees newly in leaf; the meadow grass rich in wild flowers and herbs; the myriad of insects; I love insects, their shields, metallic, copper and green, red like shiny armours; the crickets and grasshoppers with their mating calls, and the birds, yes, plenty of birds varieties; I must admit to finding it difficult to distinguish the species and never remember their names; the thick, sylvan ground of deciduous trees, the clearings of grassed-over fields interspersed amongst the woods; the expanse above, now blue, now green, now streaked in white and grey fluff ever waving and gently swinging high and low...But, alas!, where was the wide, well-trodden winding path along the down-sloping bank of the stream? Where was the stream, for that matter? Through the spider web-like intricacy of a brambles wall, I found an observation window which permitted me to meet shockingly with the devastation facing me; no stream, just a trickle of water snaking sluggishly through slime-covered stones; the foamy waterfalls and limpid, gliding sheets of water long gone. Over the opposite bank what used to be a wet meadow on the threshold of the first sway of woodland was now infested with thorny climbers of an unknown species and the dark, tall, spindly trees towering a sea of overgrown, giant briars stretching to infinity like barbed wire, drawn from one end of the stream to the road above the slopes that contained the forest, the fields, the spinneys, the hillocks, all long gone as if they could not have ever possibly existed here. The inferno I was witnessing dashed all my hopes of ever being able to retrieve my past feelings of elation when, on crossing the silvery, snaky brook and, with little difficulty, entering the woods, I walked straight into my secret den where no one used to go, sitting at the foot of a cherry or a beech, I spread all my books and, unaware and indifferent of the passing time, I spent hours on end reading and getting ready for my exams, recharging both my mental and physical batteries in the process like a solar-powered machine, except I absorbed the sun, the touch of the water as it waved past, the grass texture and its scent, the rough and smooth surface of the bark, the smell of damp undergrowth, all under the constant chirping and stridulating of birds and insects, respectively, with the odd buzz of bumble bees and the flutter of variegated butterflies. I felt alive, ecstatic and totally grounded in the self belief that such an uncontaminated beauty, such peace, such a secluded environment would stretch to the end of time. Its image etched on my mind kept me going through the toughest of times. But now, I knew I had been deceiving myself into sticking to a false ideology that it was Nature alone that had showered me with all those past seasonal delights. So, was not what was standing before my eyes right now the making of Nature? Yes, when left to its own devices...To my dismay, I fully realized for the very first time, that those well-tended meadows and fields, the clearings, the solid banks of the stream, the clean, meandering, well-delineated paths, the aptly distanced, mature trees, the undergrowth devoid of the otherwise imposing layers of decaying leaves were but the congenial outcome of human intervention. Yes, those humans, now departed, whom I despised on account of their foul attitude towards me, who certainly knew how to tend to the land but did it quietly and ceaselessly as to go unnoticed to the untrained or I'd say careless eye, just as mine had been back then. I used to enjoy an environment that, although wild in its own right, was in fact tamed by experienced hands. Whose hands were they? Peter, the farmer, Nil, the woodcutter, George, who knew how to repair and to build dry-stone walls and thus to look after the stony paths, boundaries, the stream banks and its bed. Now Nature had taken over as if in an act of revenge for having been abandoned and neglected, appallingly so, growing whatever seemed fit to cover every single inch of available ground removing the meadows and fields, spreading disorderly, expanding, chocking everything in its trail of domination and destruction by subjugation. A disaster. The death of my well-guarded, secret dream. I was truly bereaved and slowly

23

becoming conscious of a novel shattering reality I knew nothing about before. Anger assailed me and, after grabbing a sturdy stick, I started hacking my way through the wiry and thorny barrier, but in vain. The long shoots bearing thorns, some one and a half inches long, had crawled relentlessly up the boles, others dangled downwards from the top of the trees or had twisted around one another forming deadly ropes and all together they had created an impenetrable jungle of a solid rock wool net. Was I now grateful to the departed who, unbeknownst to me, had worked so hard to maintain the paradise I knew? I certainly gave them credit for their skills and perseverance but, I had still not much sympathy towards their response to my student occupation in the open air. I used to do things differently and I had the right to exist, too without having to endure their verbal abuse!

My heart at this point sank so low, that day nothing or anyone could have helped me rid myself of the sense of hopelessness that gripped my whole being. That single event marked the end of my happiness as I perceived it with nowhere to go, no secret places to hide within. Why do I need such secluded places? Well, I know I have always been an introvert and introspective person being partial to a good book rather than a party, the sounds of Nature to man-made music. It is absurd and hardly credible, but a large percentage of people these days has no ears for the natural world, so used are they to wearing ear phones in order to pour artificial sounds into their brains or to scrolling the screen of their phones. Weird, I can hear the silence of an empty room and am on cloud nine when the leaves of a poplar rustle in unison like rain drops showering a window pane. Silence, yes, the intrinsic presence of silence in the absence of everything else.

So, after the failure visit to the woodland, the mountains were my second-best and only left option. "They would provide the solution to my internal suffering," I pondered aloud. However, what did I read in some newspaper articles? The local farmers are now employing maremma dogs to fend their flocks of sheep and herds of cows off from the apparently increasing attacks of wolves. Wolves?!? They made a come back after a century in extinction; only the maremma type can face up to these fiends. It is also true though, that any dog in the wrong hands is a bad dog regardless of its breed. So I read on about three incidents in different areas in which a maremma dog has terrorized some hiking tourists and has bitten their calves. What was the advice of the Forestry Commission and the authorities in charge of the district where the farmers operate? "When you spot a maremma dog who is running in your direction (they normally weigh from 60 to 70 kg and *possess conspicuous white fangs, aside from their thick, snowy coat) stand still, do not attempt to wander off and wait".*

Wait for what, who? how long for? and why? If a maremma dog is trained appropriately, it only attacks in the event its charges are either being threatened or actively assaulted; it does not roam the mountain slopes alone in search of food from the hikers (because starved by the local shepherds) away from its territory, looking for innocent tourists to maul. But what was reported in the newspapers was now the norm and consequently I could kiss my solitary, needed mountain trips goodbye. I was so disappointed, I felt like a caged animal. I did not know what to do anymore. I felt empty:

EMPTINESS

It is a feeling deep inside,
it lays you open wide
A deep dark pool seen as a whole
I liken to my forlorn soul.

Emptiness
At its centre
lie my hopes and wishes
whilst at the periphery
are a number of intertwined thoughts
like a nest of leeches.

Emptiness
Alas! so much ferment and work ahead
can it lead to such an empty shed?
The negation of our inner, throbbing self,
like a skeptic denies the existence
of a woodland elf.

Emptiness
You read about it, drawings of it appear
but reality is nowhere near...
It cannot be measured by conventional means
it is a personal sensation that
the soul preens,
like the feathers of a bird,
the intent beak cleans.

(Della Livorno)

Emptiness... I did not know what to do anymore. Now, more than ever before I felt the urge, I was eager to get a garden, a confined space to keep out that mad world that I no longer recognized as mine. I started to seek answers to my predicament, but initially it was in vain.

The air reverberates with the local church bells which echo their vibrant tolling through the valley; it is 08:00 o' clock in the morning, the sound travels in the air to the hills and after bouncing back it dissolves like golden sand through the sparkling fingers of the sailing sun.

How distressing my discovery was, yes, finding out how over the past ten years all that was is no more, people, places, objects, all disappeared into the mists of time, only showing as fragments of memories that perhaps were just strained by my impressionable mind. What used to satisfy me, interests me no more and what used to scare me is by now a well-accepted lived experience.

"Life changes; as you age, you will understand more", my mother once or more than once told me. But in fact it's our perception of it that evolves and the more I grasp about the human race, the less sense it makes because people's erratic behaviour is just a sign of how fragile and weak humans can be. The more I live the less I understand. Is it because living to look for answers makes no sense, while living for the sake of being alive at any one point in time meets with success? Maybe in war times it does, which it is exactly what it is going on in Europe now. Why do we always seek solutions where there is no initial logic in the situations that prompt questions? I brush off these cerebral elucubrations as the last bell peel of the tower clock resonates in the air and strikes a blue-black bolt skywards. I turn in its direction and distinguish a blackbird now flying out from the middle branch of a tree. Ah, the *Turdus merula*, one of my favourite singers; its sweet, melodious notes resound near and far often playing in a well-rehearsed duetto. How delightful, how uplifting a trill, preferable in my opinion to that of a nightingale. This black lightening from the sky is one of many and yes, it evokes pleasant memories of this last spring. I can remember all too well our fortunate although unlikely moment of serendipity when, I was surprised by the frenzied twitting of hungry mouths, rising and falling with the arrival and the departure of Mother and Father. My Jasmine climber was alive with the promise of newly hatched life entering the firmament with dashes of dark velvet from branch to branch.

'If disturbed, the nest of a blackbird is abandoned by the parents and the brood is left to perish', my birdwatchers' guide solemnly states. A grave warning against human interference. Very honorable and wise a piece of advice. But Nature has its ways and animal instinct for survival is stronger than fear, I experienced one day on inspecting my climbers. Weeding amongst the bark chips is a much easier job than having to pull up unwanted vegetation from a strip of naked soil and, as I proceeded with this necessary, albeit boring task, I spotted an oval, beady object, greenish with dark speckles. Upon closer inspection, I saw a crack running along two thirds of its surface and something feebly moving, pulsating and as if trying to peep through it. There is no mistaking a foetus inside an egg. The well-formed, curved beak protruded from a bold skull and just above the former, on each side, two somewhat pronounced folds of skin surrounding shut slits. The little egg had somehow rolled out of its nest and perhaps had cracked with the impact of the fall. What to do? Pretend I did not see it and allow Nature to take its course? While pondering my quandary, a few metres away, a female blackbird sporting a brown plumage was hopping on the top of the dry-stone wall and, after stopping, she began eyeing me up and down attentively, cocking her head sideways as to assess the situation. One of her little ones was beyond recovery. How to get it back to safety? Well, I had to take a chance and under her vigilant, beady eyes, I lifted the living creature cocooned inside its shell and gently repositioned it into its nest. I moved swiftly away and carried on weeding as if nothing had happened. When I reached the end of the wall behind the Jasmine, the female was still standing on it and for a few seconds our eyes met. Those glistening, black beads rimmed with orange-golden rings seemed to convey a sense of trust and reciprocal respect. I smiled and she took to her wings darting into the thickness of the Robinia trees above. Soon afterwards, I glanced at the nest and, sure enough, she was sitting on it. Our eyes met again and I knew we had debunked a myth that, if not for this event, would have stayed with me forever. Trust Nature and it will trust you right back; this is now my motto. In a matter of days I could not believe the scene that presented itself. In exactly the same spot, not a partially cracked egg, but a featherless, little bird was lying on the bark chipped surface. A few scanty hairs were crowning its smooth head and fine, white whisps projected from each side of its beak. He lay spread-eagled as if it had splashed onto the ground in an attempted and failed Icarus's take off. But it could not be because no feather allowed such an audacious endeavour. A faint noise attracted my attention and three bold, whiskery heads rose in unison opening huge mouths like automatic clips. Then I knew, the nest narrow space had caused the little bird to fall out during the agitation that accompanied each feeding session. The unfortunate creature was still alive, its frail-looking, skinny body heaving and deflating spasmodically with each breath. This time I was confident that I should pick the bird up and place it back into the nest. On this occasion, a black-feathered male watched me, its beak dangling with fleshy morsels for his brood. Again, I moved away, slowly and methodically, to witness the Father landing on the nest to deliver his precious catch. Few seconds of high-pitched screeches, a flutter of silky feathers and the nest fell silent again. The parents momentarily gone in search of more food, I snatched a peek at the sleepy four inside their cosy hideaway, their eyelids closed shut, their heads gently quivering and rubbing against one another, falling into the soothing care of sweet slumber. A puff of wind impregnated itself with the intoxicating scent of the Jasmine blooms and I thought how lucky those little youngs were to enjoy such a dry, safe and perfumed home of their own. My presence in the garden did not seem to disturb the continuous comings and goings of both parents, who took it in turn to care for their charges.

Then, one day, out of the corner of my eye, I perceived some dark shadows with brownish nuances scuttling behind my back like small gauntlets being thrown to and fro between green robed chevaliers. Soon, the hopping fledgelings jumped out of their nest, one by one and, after taking shelter under my sage bush, they sauntered across the lawn waiting for their parents to bring earthly meals. Two days and they were gone, flown into the trees, the roofs and the sky beyond. The nest empty and silent, a reminder of how far a kind gesture can go and how more intelligent and sentient birds can be and how little credit we humans grant them. Unquestionably, but still to my surprise, I believe the same couple of birds came back four weeks later to repair their nest with a view to raise a second brood. No incident occurred this second time round but our friendship (of a different kind from that intended amongst humans) was sealed, as my very presence in the garden and toiling just below the nest did not affect their daily activities at all.

In my heart I start enjoying the pleasure of later rewarding my little friends with a bounty of red and orange berries blackbirds are known to be partial to, from my fast growing Pyracantha bushes. Without my garden I would have never experienced such intimately closed encounters with one of Nature's miracles, the birth of our native birds. What birds do my guests cherish? They sound very much pro-Nature and indeed I easily passed my message on to them that my magical realm could not be visited prior to a preliminary chat during which I would highlight my project; in this way they could appreciate the before and after intervention and express their honest opinion. Others' opinion matters, doesn't it? Of course everyone is entitled to their own, but in recent times I have witnessed too many personal ideas divested of what used to be respect and common decency; such statements devoid of any educated foundation. Speaking our minds just for the sake of often a futile and time-wasting exercise of wanting 'to join in the conversation'. How discrediting, offensive and false many comments are, only because the world has become loud , too brazen in fact for my own tastes. I am normally (and thankfully) immune to others' opinion be it negative or positive. Only erudite statements and comments can and will be taken on board. Can I expect my guests to be knowledgeable in the field of gardening? Will their comments about my garden affect my perception of them? I feel for my garden as I do for a dear friend. It rewards me in many ways and I look after it day in and day out, it is my heart and soul and its wounds are mine, I think while stroking the thick patches of cement on the wall surface by the entry gate. I have recently filled the cracks after the old plaster started crumbling a few weeks ago. I must have had a heat stroke when, under the July midday sun, during a ferocious heat wave (38 Celsius), I persevered with the filling in of the loose syenite blocks cracks in order to stabilize the walls structure.

"Are the gaps fairly wide?"

"Yes, I gauge them to be".

"Well then, you need coarse cement, five to six hours to set hard; under no rain and not in the direct sun light either which would split the newly smoothed surface".

So, I set off with a dead heavy, compact sac of coarse cement from the builders' yard to my garden. The cement powder exploded in large clouds that enveloped me and everything else in the vicinity. Mix and mix to the wanted consistency with some water from the fountain, but no bricklayer's trowel is safe in my inexperienced hands. As I tried to stick the plaster into the cracks it immediately fell onto the ground. Despair not, think of our ancestors, the so called hominids building their huts with daub and wattle. Should I just go for it and throw? Yes, I could do it. I was always a good shot. Handful of wet cement after handful filled all the holes and secured the loose, falling stones and brick shards. My heart was pounding, sweat was running down my face and back while my head was spinning by the time the job was accomplished by 16:00. Why did I not take it easy and staggered the work over a few days? Rain was forecast for the day after. Besides, I hate handling cement and when I start a demanding task, I must finish it as soon as possible. That was the second time I had to fix my walls. Was it my duty alone? Well, three of the four walls made of stone are shared with two different neighbours. I can do all the necessary repairs by myself, so why involve someone else who would invariably nose about my secret retreat? Yes, let's keep it as hidden as I possibly can from everyone but a few trustworthy people in order to preserve this splendid aura of celestial beauty. Amongst the few people I trust are, needless to say, my guests-to-be. Will the latter appreciate all the hard work that has gone into the repairing, upkeep, designing and planting of this green paradise? Any uncalled for comments or annoying questions I shall brush aside; only gratitude for their initial gesture will occupy my mind.

What they did for me was life changing and totally positive. There is a kind of spiritual karma, of a transcendental nature that binds this garden to me. How it came to be mine beggars belief and there are the extremely unusual circumstances that make me stand in awe of it right now as I feel the same kind of breezy atmospheric environment that transfixed me back then. Suddenly, out of the corner of my eye, a frayed flag flashing red and yellow and deep orange, fluttering, waving in the breeze as it caught the rays of the late morning sun and autumn flames were burning the flank of the hill. The dog was pulling on the leash, too much, I harnessed him back a bit. Where was I? Rows and rows of crimson canvasses billowing and flattening with the breath of the wind. Or were they blades already tinted vermillion with the passage of time? Fiery and golden butterflies, swerving, floating, hesitating before circling and eventually laying down on their mortal bed. The wavy melee of brilliant colours stood out of the sluggish, lengthening shadows below the brow of the hill. I love the Fall as red as blood, page after page it explodes into a painter's palette as its principal protagonists meet with their relentless demise. So much beauty hit my senses like a dart to my heart. I turned around and, instead of the familiar steep bend in the road, I remember seeing images of avenues flash through my mind. Rows of mature sugar maples trees swaying their rich canopies in the wind; the large leaves flying high in the sky like kites tethered to a thin thread, their fragile stalks almost devoid of sap; the tannins, having accomplished their masterpieces on these aerial canvasses displayed a masterful blend of multi-coloured, stunning hues and were now witnessing a specialized layer of cells (abscission layer) aided by the presence of the auxine hormone to perform the act of severing the leaves' lives from their parent tree. Only then, the feeble attachment would relinquish its hold on the twig, at the touch of a wind puff, the swift race of a squirrel through the branches, the drops of a gentle autumn drizzle, or simply the papery weight surrendering its frame to the pull of gravity. Mesmerized, I used to observe the spectacle first from a distance, then strolling along the park snaky paths, from near and at last by standing under the myriad of painted flags swerving, quivering or just hanging out in the balance of Nature to meet up with their creator once again. The slanting rays of the twilight set the leaves ablaze with tones of red, copper, orange, deep yellow and variegated shades of green. The canopies now resembled large umbrellas, be-jewelled with sparkling gems while at the foot of the mossy and lichen covered boles, a widely spread, dappled, flamboyant counterpane was flaunting some gaudy tints of the rainbow. I could not think of anything more peaceful, attractive and introspective than being domed by a maple tree in the height of Fall. By then, the English countryside where I had my home was sliding into a melancholic languor, through the passage of the seasons from summer to autumn and then winter. Along the crest of the far away low hills that surrounded our residential area, every day that went by saw a new colour exploding now as fast as lightening, now more slowly, in all its beauty as the Robinias, Maples, Beech, Silver birches started to don their festive clothes in view of the celebrations for the end of the summer and into the harvest season, with a refulgent gesture of triumph before the rain, wind and mud brought their joyous lives to an abrupt, undignified but ineluctable death. I picked up one leaf that had lightly drifted to the ground, touching the surface with the delicate sound of a sheet of paper landing onto the floor. It was one of the most gorgeous gifts of Nature I had ever seen, a seven-lobed leaf spread out like the palm of an open hand. The top lobe markedly taller than the rest and deep sinuses in between each crested lobe. A sturdy midrib running longitudinally the whole length of the leaf from which several veins departed to mark the tip of each lobe and giving rise to a thick network of minor, finer veins throughout the surface of both the lower and upper pages, thus dividing it into several fragmented portions of differing size equal to the wings of a butterfly when observed against the light, where the carotenoid and flavonoid pigments, now predominant on the fading chlorophyll compound, produced works of art by the strokes of invisible brushes operating in the secrecy of chilly, Fall nights. I held the leaf between my fingers for what felt like an interminable time but which in fact was but a few minutes (two or three?) while I was showered by several other sisters of hers that floated, swirled, dived and at last touched down with inexorable pity, wrapped in their capes of ephemeral beauty. All around me an identical display of Nature was taking place, the large leaves of the grape vines climbing the fence by the road, staring at the passing traffic with dark, green faces, smeared in crimson blotches like herpes sufferers, while others with coppery eyelids, half devoured by blight, agitated their golden margins, old masks battered by the elements whose outer, precious frames were tenaciously holding on, their tendrils now lignified in a grip of steel. More leaves were falling now as the sun, after sailing into the western horizon, had disappeared in a pool of kaki juice. I would certainly press this leaf and, after varnishing it with transparent sealant, would keep it forever.

Yes, I still have it, looking as gorgeous as it did back then. As I hold it by its petiole, it rekindles the passion elicited by the very moment it landed at my feet and the surreal scenery that, that autumn afternoon regaled to form an indelibly precious memory. The memory that re-surfaces whenever a detail, a scent, a particularly impressive hue transports me back to the special day, one of many, certainly, but one which more than most stimulated my perception of blissful happiness.

"Is it where you live? Really?

"Yes, turn left into the close and drive up to the two bollards ahead, please," I instructed the taxi driver who had driven me all the way from London into the heart of the Hampshire countryside one September day, early in the afternoon.

"You are very lucky, my lady, I envy you!" he uttered passionately while surveying and absorbing the spectacular show of the maples avenue opposite our drive. The wind had picked up and ominous black clouds were rolling in from the west, causing a storm of strikingly bright coloured leaves to fill the sky, spiraling up and up, carried by the whipping air currents, before descending like out-of-control gliders onto the surrounding area, some transported yards away or disappearing into nothingness altogether. The stretch of lawn along our drive was slowly being layered with a multitude of dazzling hues, a phantomatic weaving machine interlacing a dramatic, wavy cloth. I paid and tipped the driver, thanking him for the pleasant journey. Some time afterwards, I looked through my bedroom window while the *rain drops, at first hefty and sparse then thick and fast, fell varnishing afresh the leafy cloth, accentuating its already riotous brilliance further; and I also noticed a few yards along the drive, the taxi still lingering, however, on this occasion not waiting for the next customer but, no doubt, with the driver's nose glued to the car window, savouring the wonder he was witnessing and which continued to unfold.*

In the wake of such moving memories, I felt the urge to explore the area surmounted by the iridescent canopies which, like then, held an irresistible appeal. I, therefore, decided to venture through the main road of the village above, from which several alleyways branch out and slope down from the hill I could see where I stood with the dog. The day after we took the turn onto Roma street and walked on till, instinctively I believe, I knew which path could take me to the wooded ledge I was after. I strolled along till I came across a lady who was leaving her gated property. We exchanged a few words and I learnt I could reach the sylvan area directly from the road below the hill, so on that occasion I turned back and later did as instructed to realize what an intricate maze of footpaths spidered across the slope. It was only the year after, in the late summer that I ventured once again through the alleyway off the main village road in search of the early glimpses of the Fall to come. I started to take a few hesitant steps into the passage squeezed in between two rows of ancient habitations. The smell of damp rising from their foundations and the rich colonies of green lichen through the fissures of the kerb, a sure revelation redolent of history, along with the round and smooth river rocks sticking out the crumbling plaster of the rickety walls. Where the medieval dwellings came to an abrupt end, the path became enclosed by tall, grey, dry-stone walls and meandered descending towards the very spot I was after, the brow of the hill, just above the road where only the year before I was standing with the dog and which I had reached from the opposite side of the hill at the bottom of which stands a 12th century church by a rushing stream which could be heard murmuring as it quickly tumbled, as an affluent, into the main, larger water course further ahead. As I slowly proceeded along the uneven, cobbled way with tall, disheveled grasses and wind-seeded wild flowers, here and there on both sides, confident I was within reach of the source of the dazzling colours I was longing for, since I started to spot a golden flag or two trembling in the breeze, I now hastened my pace and my eyes caught a passing glimpse of something hidden through the grey curtain of syenite blocks; a secret glory beckoned to me beyond a crack where, in the stifling, heavy haze of the very late summer afternoon, a gentle zephyr agitated the silvery green sprays of a large prostrated lavender bush, busy bees dancing all around it, while an emerald green grass pointed to a gloriously firm stance of a mirror image syenite wall on the other side. Shade provided by the luscious canopies above from which a number of oblong, large, yellowing pears swang shily amongst the quivering fronds. What lied beyond my peeping hole was a slice of the natural world which had been snatched away for private use. It felt secretive, screened away from preying eyes, a green space enclosed within four walls, I thought. A square of terrestrial crust belonging to someone, longing to belong or simply to be left to be. My head was reeling, I was overwhelmed by the emotion one experiences when privy to a forbidden object of desire. Now I knew what Tantalus might have gone through as he reached for fruit and water that kept eluding him. I felt starved, too of a sheltered, quiet and natural, green place where I could let go of all my preoccupations and ground myself to attain that level of mental balance that had thwarted me for a long time. Engrossed in my thinking I took two steps away from the hole towards the crown of the hill and proximal to the crack, slightly recessed into the wall as if to go unnoticed, more alluring still was a tall, narrow, metal gate, its bottle green paint an absolute shadow of its past shiny self, rusty hinges and an ancient lock conjured up all the memories and emotions associated with a secret place lying beyond these prohibitive iron bars. I was attracted to the gaps between the bars like a magnet because they afforded me a much wider view than that provided by the hole in the wall. My eyes were met with a little bare garden, only the lavender bush alive with the breath of a gentle breeze and a square cover of freshly mowed grass. It felt like a perfect place for me, because at the point where the gate stood, the cobbled path dropped abruptly with a series of crude, uneven and heavily subsided syenite steps, thus focusing the attention of any passerby on their own gait to avoid tripping or falling rather than paying attention to a faded, well camouflaged iron gate in the wall. Yes, that was it. I remember well and my mind keeps wandering to that fateful day. Although at the end of summer, the sky was a sheet of scorching metal reflecting a suffocating heat back to earth, Nature stood silent in that searing cauldron, when I found myself taking a short cut through the shaded alleyway between two red-hot, dry-stone walls. My pace was slow and meditative as if I were hesitating in the heat before plunging into the shade of the low, bowing fronds ahead. I looked around and saw nothing but the sky, the approaching canopies and the uninterrupted, speckled greyness of these syenite walls; it was only then that my stupor was disturbed by that break in the scene, there it was, beyond the stone blocks and their haphazard cracks, a window into a different world, a hidden world, beyond that faded, unassuming gate. A gate, an entry point which delimited the public area from a private one which could not be trespassed. My heart missed a beat when I stopped cautiously, transfixed. I knew I had to act on my discovery, I felt like an impetus, a surge of courage, spurred by a deep need to possess that little square of our planet. That very need had been lying dormant for four years, but just as life itself, my desire was unstoppable. I am sure that day I heard a voice wooing me inside. Maybe it was the wind or just a figment of my imagination; my inner craving to partake in the sanctity of life preset, pulsating behind that wall. I knew deep inside whose voice it was, yes, it was the Spirit's of the Place, the Genius's Loci, or the archetypal Green Man's, charming me into its fascinating world. I had to oblige lest I spent what was left of my life wondering what happiness really meant to me. Because happiness is but a state of mind, a fleeting moment, caught on the wings of a butterfly, on the light of a glowworm on the wavy motion of a falling leaf seized by a puff of wind. It lasts long enough to create an instant memory which, in a flash, becomes relegated to the past. Only rekindled emotions can retrieve that perceived happiness to be lived again for a mere instant. That paradise behind the wall, however, is a constant presence and it evolves, peaks, dies down and is reborn, ready to resurrect its beauty from the ashes of winter in a continuous rhythm which inspires the most powerful of human attributes, hope.

These sweet memories prompt me to open the gate and step into that very alleyway that led me to my present state of full contentment, while I enjoy the fruits of my labour to share with my imminent guests. Today, like one year ago, the stony steps with their rough surface, lumpy cobbles and subsided edges are taking me through a dark arch of overgrown bramble, towered by the airy canopies of giant Robinias. After sloping down one yard, it bends to the left along a dilapidated fence, to come out into the open, commanding an anticipated view of the forested valley below and the hills that rise from the latter. A truly idyllic spot. Then, on the right, there they are! The flags of golden and kaki hues swaying in the wind. I stand below the canopies of these boles which, like before, are welcoming autumn to wink its next arrival, gold and russet through the hailing branches of the false Acacia trees, and I am truly mesmerized. This is obviously a miracle of Nature that repeats itself, punctually. I walk back into my garden and this time I close the gate behind me. I am aware of the Spirit right inside here, indeed even the air is different between the passageway and my plot as the walls that enclose it create a micro climate just as they do in any green garden of England I knew, including my own.

Presently the taxi would fetch us to take us to our last English destination before we flew out to Italy long term, a countryside Bed and Breakfast. It was May, the loveliest of months when the gardens and the countryside alike look their best dressed in flowery frocks of green silk.

The tall french windows of the kitchen that used to be the gateway into my garden were now firmly locked, the keys with our estate agent. A glass barrier had risen between my garden and I. While I used to love the large panes through which during inclement weather I could still enjoy my green outdoors space, I now considered them my antagonists as my perception was shifting fast, my formal habitual portal into beatitude had disappeared before my very eyes leaving me with a yawning gap, a sense of unbridgeable longing for something that used to be mine and which I loved unconditionally.

"Would you like to step into the garden now? As you see it is just over the threshold of this very spacious and bright kitchen. Next to it is the utility room with its west-facing door giving a secondary access to the garden."

The building manager unlocked the double french windows and I stepped out into the one hundred and fifty square metres of newly turfed lawn bound by a tall, wooden palisade sitting on a concrete skirting wall on three sides.

"This is going to be my sweet, concealed retreat when I am home from work". The neighbouring more mature trees and shrubs were hanging over the top of our property as in an effort to oblige us with some shade besides conferring a well established landscaped look.

"I love it. It is virgin soil, full of promise for the future," I replied to the eager estate manager. He matched my enthusiasm with a large approving smile. That episode occurred fifteen years before when we had just moved from Leicestershire, down south to purchase a bigger property as an investment for our future. Now that investment has come to fruition, it has paid off and, although financially we have achieved our aim, spiritually and emotionally I felt deprived, even bereaved by the loss of our beloved garden. From the bottom step of the staircase, I sat in silence, fully aware of this very last chance to absorb my sad, present reality. I scanned the kitchen through its open door, its emptiness as poignant as the state of my mind, regret and pity ran in tandem from one recess of my conscience to the next, seeking desperately a gleam of solace in the decision to sell our property.

My heart was pounding in my chest with sheer excitement while my husband stirred our car around the corner of our new residential estate. At the end of a private drive by two black bollards rose our brand new, four bedroom detached house in the middle of the gorgeous Hampshire countryside. The land onto which the estate had been built, belonged to a farmer and fields of wheat and oats used to roll like the waves in the sea by the touch of the breeze where our house now stood. In earlier times smoke used to rise from the round huts of a neolithic settlement, later occupied by the Romans, the ancient origins fully researched and documented by Wessex archeology during the excavations for the conversion of farmland into building land. The rich history dating back to 6000 BC intrigued me since I am passionate about early humans' lives.

Before reaching our house we spotted the two removal vans already parked there and five men frantically unloading our large boxes of belongings and carrying them inside the new house. This was going to be our home for a number of years, but I knew deep inside that all that, one day, would come to an end, but now I wanted to live in the present and I was determined to enjoy it.

How hopeful and truly happy I felt back then, I reminisce. I walked through the main entrance, took a peek at the wide, balustraded, white staircase, then gingerly carried on into the kitchen to step immediately into by now, my own garden. A gentle breeze met me with approval as the palisade fencing started to cast its long shadows across the lawn while the neighbour's overhanging trees were sporting the first yellow leaves rimmed with crimson and dotted with bronze spots. It was the beginning of September and autumn was already in the air with its colours, its fruitfulness, its cool breezes and towering black clouds rolling in from the south. How atmospheric, how languid and totally abandoning my feelings were.

"Nice house, madam, really! And the garden a perfect match, a green extension to your house. Will you design and plant it yourself?"

How revealing, I thought, that the removal people guessed I might be the type of person to both design and plant this garden, my own, personal garden, my slice of paradise to enjoy and nurture through the seasons.

How many delightful hours I spent under our tall cherry tree, writing, drawing, painting, admiring its grey bark, fitting its slim bole like a glove. Few cherries ever ripened fully, through the greed of impulsive blackbirds that preferred a sour fruit than no fruit at all. I had picked the seedling at a National Trust property ten years before, its fronds now fingering the panes of the upstairs bedroom window.

Now I could only watch with welling eyes the black limbs crawling on the bare kitchen walls, inching their way along, to snap up suddenly before resuming a calmer countenance of stroking the surface of the room which lied empty and desolate. These limbs like the hairy legs of a giant black spider, felt like a desperate attempt by my cherry tree to attract my attention, to demand an explanation as to why we were departing taking everything with us but leaving it behind, all alone, standing there, to agitate its fronds before the window and cast a shadow on the walls in a last, desperate effort to be rescued from its doubtful destiny. My heart ached and, for a brief moment I felt despair. I did not want to leave that property, the time to move on which I knew would come one day, was upon me right there and then; totally unprepared for the change it felt heavy, menacing, scary, like a sledgehammer beating down on my head, driving me crazy and I could not even hug my beloved tree goodbye. I knew I had to go to leave that life behind for a brand new one abroad. The move would be dramatic, but compensated for by the ancestral house and Alpine village I grew up in.

Is this what I will experience when my life comes to an end? I wonder... Likewise I knew all too well one day I would have to die, to leave everything, everything behind. And yet, although aware of my ineluctable destiny, would I be unprepared, unwitting, scared even to turn my back to all that had been familiar to me up to that fatal moment? Yes, I felt I was dying; I never believed I could grow so fond of this garden, the extension to my English home, my British life with my dreams, accomplished projects and hopes for the future. That place has grown inside me like the roots of my cherry tree pushed their way into the soil, branching out in search of nutrients and a means to anchor itself upright into this square of the universe. But, unlike my tree my roots are atavic and my free will of an able-bodied person allows me to move to far away lands, to be psychologically uprooted without suffering the consequences my tree would have to endure, if I were to take it to Italy with me. Perish the thought! Although I possessed a large three-storeys ancient house, I had no garden of my own there! A sinking sensation assailed me and gripped my innards like the steely jaws of a vice. Only now it dawned upon me that in two days' time and for possibly a countless number of years, I would have to make do without a garden. But how? My rational thinking was questioning my decision to sell this property even more inquisitively and pressingly now. Yes, what about my beloved garden? The house in Italy stands within a medieval, communal courtyard, that although spacious, airy and friendly, is not mine alone. Yes, there is a nice patio with a rockery in front of the entrance, but as for privacy and disguise, the reality was far from reassuring. My mind tricked me into the memories of my childhood and several past summer holidays in my native land which form idyllic images of green meadows, bubbling brooks, tinkling rivulets, extensive deciduous woodland, hills and rocky ledges, all free to roam and enjoy as if my own reserved land. The vision of my past life in the Alps, playing before my eyes, somewhat soothed my pain and gave me hope for a bright future that I was prepared to accept after my loss. Of course, back then I did not know that nothing could have been further from the truth and that it was that very adverse change that led me to where I am now, sitting in my lovely garden, waiting for my friendly visitors to come.

Dusk fell onto the garden, and the white-washed kitchen walls became grey and dull. The wait for the time to leave for good was drawing to a close. I gathered all my strength and stood on two shaky legs that slowly dragged me to the french windows. I glued my nose to the cold panes and fixed my look into the darkening recesses of that green square. The rosemary, sage and lavender bushes looked magnificent along with the little ash trees and sweet chestnut tree, which I had grown from a germinating nut I had left in the fridge, forgotten, after roasting the bulk of fruit I had bought at Tesco's. Some climbing rose shoots were about to bloom and the rows of spring flowers consisting of, hyacinths, tulips, anemones and narcissi were all open sporting their brilliant colours even now that the sun had set behind the fence. At the foot of my adorable cherry tree was a coronet of yellow crocuses interspersed with blue ones which were about to fade; some had already done so, as if in sympathy with my anguished mind. I remember the day I purchased them at Lidl's and the joy I felt while planting them and later watching them open their petals under the gentle touch of spring.

The doorbell! I jolted out of my languishing reverie into which I had fallen and which had transported me into a deliciously happy period of my existence. My heart heavy with grief, I walked away from the windows and, as I was leaving the kitchen I lifted my eyes towards the, by now, indistinguishable cupboards faintly silhouetted on the walls and at that point I seemed to make out a hand shape waving goodbye. Perturbed, I turned around and perceived a leafy branch of my cherry agitated by the wind, saluting me for the very last time. Fast now, I strode along the corridor, grabbed my bag, opened the door to my husband and the taxi driver and, with a swift movement shut and locked the entrance door before jumping into the car. That door, as I think of it, felt as heavy and inexorable as the lid of a coffin being sealed for eternity. My British life was locked away forever. The taxi drove off and the two men became deeply engrossed in jolly conversation while I was looking through the window and saw, nothing. Only one thought had entered and was now gnawing at my mind: I had no garden any more! The move from Britain was swift and uneventful, just as it had always been on our holidays, except on this occasion I was under no illusion that this was no holiday at all as, instead of producing the illustrated guide of the Aosta Valley, the same day of our arrival we started moving the furniture about making space for the three hundred odd boxes that the pantechnicon was about to deliver. The words stress and exhaustion were growing out of all proportion and sadly, were marring what should have been a happy come back.

Yes, what a day that was, it feels like decades ago but in fact it only goes back four years. I have certainly come a long way in a short space of time and this amazing garden in which I am standing now is the evidence of my success.

Through the feathery canopies of the slender Robinias over my garden fence I see blue glints, fragments of sky, flashes of sun rays as if redirected from a mirror, dancing, now showing, now gone in an intermittent wave, a quivering lace engendered by the incandescent disk of the sun, like the shimmering surface of a calm, distant sea. A thousand sherds of a shattered looking glass sparkling blindingly. Up in the air, the diaphanous opalescence of a myriad of specs, life darting haphazardly in the shaft of light, a mimicry of the frenzied madness enveloping the world like a chocking pall. Meanwhile, birds swing gently on the power lines, now on the nearest one, then on the one further away, beaks wriggling with live prey. Presently they dive onto the ground and hop defiantly under my scrutiny, towards the rosemary pot. A brief flutter of their wings land them on to the swaying branches of the plum tree. The Ivy wall comes alive with greedy twits, then, silence falls again. Some nests hidden amongst the thick leafage? Maybe Mother and Father, these birds dutifully, methodically, constantly feed their young with continuity and order, giving hope to the eye of the observer. Stability perseveres in the natural world, it is almost tangible despite the environmental upheavals. It seems that chaos belongs to humans along with almost predictable instability spreading throughout the sick planet. The inquisitive black beads, flickering, as they go about their business, these birds offer a glimpse into their trusting soul. They seem to know a limpid mind, they check and observe for mischief and intention. Their instinct does not betray them. It looks like some humans may still be capable of niceties and kindness...

The sparkling beauty of this special morning is marked by the melodious chime of the bells, the ninth hour has struck. The sun is slowly sailing from the east towards its zenith where it will be almost perpendicular to the turf on which I am standing, flooding the entire garden with blinding light.

What a contrast, what a scene, as day gives way to night and the world (this part of the world) goes to bed. Who would guess the sheer transformation, like a stage of stunning costumes when the lights are slowly dimmed to obscurity, we know the colours and shapes are still there but we can no longer distinguish them from their background and must hone our remaining senses, only then we'll be satisfied with the presence of what we previously witnessed. That scene occurred precisely one evening at nine o' clock. The village had already donned a heavy bluish cape conveying the impression that autumn was on its way ready to knock on my door. A thick and grey layer of stationary clouds was trapping the radiating heat of the summer day including the inferno rising from the freshly tarmacked road. A visit to my garden was imperative since rain had, thankfully, been forecast for the next following few days. By nine thirty I was about to turn into the cobbled way that from the little 12th century octagonal church leads up a winding mule path to our garden. We slowly started the snaky ascent treading on loose stones and trying to avoid small depressions in the ground, of these well worn-down, smooth syenite cobbles and dressed blocks that served as steps. The night was very warm, but as we advanced, my husband and I, up the wooded hill, we experienced a marked difference in air currents. The fresh breeze from the stream bed whose impetuous, foamy waters tumble amongst rocks and boulders as a tributary of the main valley's larger stream and the crisp draught that is channeled through the gorge of the nearby mountain and is carried down the plain, racing past hillocks, outcrops, wood clearings and the sparse habitation to hit the varying degrees of canopy thickness and the bending angle of the heavy boughs over our track. The fresh air mixing with the warmer atmosphere produced an intoxicating scent of cut grass, Jasmine inflorescences, sweet chestnut and thick vegetation of mixed origin which traveled in concentric wafts that perfumed the area like a bottled botanical fragrance, a romantic spritz for the summer days. The last steep climb up the stone stairway, through the undergrowth damp with moisture from the covering trees, proved to be a revelation to our eyes. The waning gibbous moon a mere sliver of silver glint in the sky illuminated faintly the upper margin of some fluffy sparse clouds which, as night fell, were trapping the city artificial lights thus reflecting them back to earth (the visible consequences of light pollution). The result was a subdued darkness, where every object around us was discernable but did not cast a shadow of itself anywhere to be noticed. Then, suddenly, unexpectedly, round the bend of the path on top of the steep climb on our right-hand side, like the very first time, we spotted a darker recess in the wall and there it was, the iron gate, the entrance to our garden. No longer the faded, bottle green, skeletal, narrow gate of a year ago, but a full-bodied, grass-green, freshly-varnished entry way, like a tree in leaf, now wearing a double white and yellow shawl on its back, bedecked with a fake leaf apron at the front, an effective concealment of what lied behind its ghostly-like presence, and a far cry from its see-through skinny outlook of the previous summer. Like a doorman mounting guard over the threshold to our private room. I could not suppress a smile. As we stared in contemplation, I meticulously observed the tall, curved, dry-stone wall that delimits the garden from the public pathway where we were standing now: it towered weathered and proud, protective like the battlements of an ancient medieval castle. The potted Sedum capped with red blooms, nestled on the base of the stone column capital, a flag of ownership and well-defined character of this place. We turned the key in the lock, pushed open the gate that greeted us with a clunky noise and upon stepping beyond the entrance, we immediately shut it closed with a thud and, with a swift turn of the key on the other side of the key hole, we locked it back firmly as if in a gesture to protect ourselves from any potential intruder who might shutter our dreamy state of mind. The gates garbs fell back into place, respectfully, in order to safeguard our need for privacy. The grasshoppers and crickets, with an unrivalled frenzy, conscious of the passage of time that dissipates the chance of passing their genes onto the next generation, were rasping and stridulating the night away. Few pipistrelles dived down into the advancing obscurity, fluttering their membranous wings frantically, as if to negotiate some suspended obstacle, invisible to our eyes. The mellifluous wind rustled the topmost fronds of the trees looking down on us, their black, leafy fingers tickling the sky. The solar lamps next to the wall-mounted looking glass were lit with a cold, opaque and contained energy which, through their own reflection, opened the view into an extended, twin realm over the threshold of the grey stonewall. It was a magic door into a parallel world where only my imagination could travel. There I felt safe, protected from the encumbrances of the present, chaotic living that I reject and abhor. There, the feeble flame of a citronelle candle, emitting its flickering, warm glow from a transparent glass jar, represented an expansion of the natural environment which I was striving to preserve alongside the one I had just created with plants, trees and garden furnishing. The flame was like the soul of the earth, the light emanated from the Spirit of the Place, the insects, invertebrates, tiny mammals and all the vegetation around me, that enveloped me and permeated my being to become one with me. There was nothing eerie about the darkness that had fallen in the garden: the latter felt at peace, asleep under a blanket of gentle dew and a veil of black organza, both descended from the sky. All was quiet, no lights from the road nor from the houses could reach us, only the thin wedge of the moon radiance and the stars twinkle were visible in the celestial vault. I lied down on the damp, cool grass and listened. The customary birds songs, chainsaws, passersby' conversations and neighbouring chatter, along with the roaring of motorbikes that unexpectedly fill the air at intervals, all had died down. I strained my ear to interpret any other sound above the whirring, grating maracas of the serenading crickets. Silence pervaded the night but, as I refined my awareness, I was privy to the soft dialogue between the stream and the leaves of the forested hillock where our garden is nestled. They spoke a language unknown to me that went beyond the usual sounds of the natural world. The experience humbled me and suggested the irrepressible life power of Nature versus the cognizant, destructive force of humanity who ravage the planet including their own existence despite being aware of the consequences. From the depth of the thick, black canopies I perceived a light sighing and rustling interrupted by the cricking and rattling noise of the upright boughs rubbing past one another in their slow, swinging movement. Their voices were heard by the stream that echoed, its incessant roaming over boulders and mossy banks, now rushing with impetus, now gliding with silvery fingers before tumbling below the arched, cobbled bridge by the church. They talked eagerly through the night, who knows what about? Then their whispers became intermingled with the crickets' and the breeze, as they came into my mind they died away into the recesses of time. Presently only the crickets were audible while the wind changed its direction, their sand-filled musical instruments, and the highly annoying high pitched buzzing of the mosquitoes. The night had now spread its black wings upon us and, it was time to make a move back home as, despite the solar lamps, we had plunged into the pitch-black darkness. All candles snuffed out and chairs put away, we unlocked our magic gate to step out into the folds of the night where our cobbled path lies during daylight. We walked in single file guided by the beam of a bright torch and a few steps on we reached the first habitation at the end of the alleyway illuminated by a single lamp post. The sight of the street ahead with the signs of human presence through the glowing slits of the bolted shutters induced a state of anxiety, an expectation of potential evil arising from behind the locked doors. A noticeable paradox with the peaceful and calm mindfulness afforded me by the sounds of Nature rising into the growing blackness of the witching hour. My *insecurity was further precipitated by the dancing shadow of a long, branching creeper that fanned its way free-fall along the wall, extending its deformed limits into the alleyway under the spell of the wind. The shadows swelled and abated with the puffs and pants in the heat of the summer thus cooling down those desperate climbers in the grip of the persisting drought. The several lampposts of the silent, main street greeted me benevolently and infused a warm sensation of domesticity. Then something melodious attracted my attention, a sound I had never noticed before, which now filled the stillness of the night rising inside my consciousness to remind me of its primordial force, it was the water of the stone fountain splashing into its vat. It sparkled silvery as it gushed out of its metal spout and plunged noisily in concentric ripples distorting the heavens above. It was a familiar sound which got dampened by the constant traffic and human jangling during the day, thus drumming away in a sotto voce existence. Now, set in its voiceless road recess, in the dimness of the night, the fountain was singing aloud, supreme and clear, its notes stroking the breeze which, happy to oblige, carried them far away up and down the street as to announce a prelude to a dreamy, lyric crescendo elevating itself into the firmament. I stood before it in awe of its artistic gift which was unbeknownst to anyone, but to those who seek out hidden* beauty in the average daily life. The morning after, the long shadow of the recently departed night, seemed to linger a bit longer as the flaming, blazing summer disk started tracing its course along the pale opalescent vault. Dullness gave soon way to brightness as the radiance burst into being, now shining high in the east and the last of the darkness's sleepy eyes opened into a glorious sunny day. It is an absolute truth that every time I enter my garden and close the gate behind me, I perform a ritual act of shutting the world out, in order to fully enjoy a very private place. I feel embraced by the spirit of whatever season is manifesting at that point in time, confident that the following season will come along, never disappointing me it being summer or winter, the latter with the promise of cooler temperatures and a welcome gentle flurry of rain or snow that makes my heart throb with joy. I can then anticipate the growth of fragrant plants, the quivering leaves, the chirping birds and crickets, features that carry on well into the dead of autumn. I feel protected by the surrounding ancient stone walls as if I had entered a fortress, a forbidden room of my own. It is a magical atmosphere where time stands still and loses its contemporary meaning of dictating one's daily chores and obligations. Inside my garden I abandon myself in either the slow or fast pace of Nature which hastens in the height of spring by a sexually-driven frenzy of reproductive aims, to deflate in the summer with a lusciousness of ripening fruits and eventually tired-out living organisms, welcoming the Fall as a time of respite and recuperation before the sleep of winter, with an infallible rhythm. Here, within these sacred four walls the only true value is the sanctity of irrepressible life and its cyclical cadence. Here time is marked by the seasonal changes, by the instinct of survival by competing for sun, water, nutrients, space and hence fulfill the essential urge of encompassing universal love. Yet, all these life's demands go unnoticed to the eye of those unaware and only harmony of shape, colour, fragrance, movement and sound intermingling now, domineering then, now meek and unassuming but intermittently pre-potent and modest, is observed or passively absorbed and enjoyed. Only the savvy can fully appreciate Nature's struggles and such struggles can be mitigated with targeted intervention which I try to aptly put in place. My garden is a haven of spiritual peace and unparalleled personally experienced artistry. I honestly could no longer live without it. The more I live my garden the more convinced I become I was correct in thinking that it was imperative to protect rather than destroy the local fauna of my green paradise, under the hospices of the Green Man whose disgorging leafy and fruity mask lies under a glass bell by the entry gate. No plant, herb, flower or tree has been damaged by the rich variety and number of animal species thriving in my garden. Centipedes, millipedes, slugs, snails, libellulas, butterflies, honey bees, carpenter bees, ladybirds, earthworms, lizards, moles to name but a few, dwell in symbiosis with my plant life and keep the soil well drained and fertile. It is a prosperous and happy home.

"You have had no moles in your plot?"

"Not really", I lie in reply to my incredulous neighbour.

He does not know how beneficial they are and their earthy extrusions can be seen to, very quickly indeed. Vibrating deterrents can be employed, too with no harm to the lovely tunnel diggers. According to the previous owners, now my guests of honour-to-be in this glorious morning, my beautiful garden sported several mole hills all over the grass; briar shoots were growing underneath the fence, pricking the ground with steely spears and the self-seeded grass was growing as fast as lightening followed by thunder. Andrea was entrusted with his own judgement as to when his gardening skills were to be implemented by peeping regularly through the gate. He would employ his strimmer to cut the grasses down to a yellow and brown mottled ground surface similar to a scalp suffering from alopecia on the way to recovery. Obviously, such hazardous, drastic interventions did the lawn no good and severe bald patched dotted the area in turn. The luxuriant, emerald green, velvety turf I am enjoying now, a far cry from its former sick self. The two, seventy and one hundred litres respectively water tubs, had seen little precipitation when I took possession of the plot and contained a thick volume of black and slimy sludge giving off the whiff of seasoned gangrene, before being rolled down the hill with the dual purpose of ridding them of their offensive insides and of taking a purifying plunge into the chilly currents of the stream down below. Now empty and easily moved, they were placed by the wall which delimits my property from the neighbour's hens shelter. It was not long before some heavy and persistent storms, filled the round-bellied tubs to their brims. Then, one day, they were joined by a stray friend that had been lying in waiting by an abandoned allotment in the nearby village. Darker and bluer in colour compared with the other two, the three of them formed the perfect picture of a happy household on a family camping trip, holding pot-bellies of different sizes. 'Isn't that a familiar scene while walking the streets these days?' I chuckled to myself. Later in the year as their clean, transparent looks became blotched with black spots that defaced their beauty, they were forced to conceal themselves under a doubly folded organza veil originating from mosquitoes nets, pulled tight and tied down around their fat necks with heavy, colourful strings. Now their happiness and my wellbeing, truth to be told, were literally sealed. As father, mother and child bedecked in white lace stood elegantly by the entrance to the garden, guarding their stinging secrets and drowning them for our own sake. I am sure my visitors will appreciate my clever device and I can bet they will comment on it.

There are many ways to embellish an otherwise essential but ugly object in the garden also keeping away pests as you go. This is where creativity is fuelled more by necessity than artistic prowess. That was my primary concern from the very beginning, yes water, as the fundamental element of any successful garden was lacking. No running water tap, hose or well in the plot. The only source, the stream, far too distant and at the foot of the hill through a snaky, cobbled path. However, blessed by luck as I am, the singing-open-vat-stone-fountain at the end of the alleyway which leads to my garden, is open for business full time. So the above was the only option worthwhile considering.

"Haven't you read the town hall notices? They have been affixed under the portico".

I anxiously learnt that due to the prolonged winter and spring drought no water could be collected from the public fountains to soak either vegetables patches or gardens. Panic! And now what? I had just planted a few specimens and in order to establish themselves they needed regular watering. I, nevertheless, filled my twenty litres watering can from the fountain and plodded back towards the alleyway entrance. No sooner had I been warned by this villager, than one of her neighbours nonchalantly walked out of her courtyard holding her watering can, she filled it and was warmly greeted by the law-abiding villager. 'So unusual for an Italian', I pondered, who let her walk away without passing any comment on the transgressive action. Was that an example of the so-called conspiracy of silence? Or complacent attitude towards a well-respected friend who was flouting the rules unchallenged? 'Blow it! Challenge me again if you dare'. I sent my only English-speaking husband to fill the can again and, as I anticipated he got told off, too. However, he courteously replied: "Have a good day", plastered a toothy green on his face and went on filling the can to its full capacity. The second time he went on his mission he was left alone, perhaps both his accent and teeth exposure had guarded off our valiant villager. As it goes, the three proud tubs, by hook or by crook are the life line of the garden with the helping hand by Sister fountain. My visitors knew of the difficulties involved in keeping a garden alive and I believe, that's the reason they never grew anything and never developed this plot. Will they be surprised now? Will they regret selling me the land that came with the house? I would not sell my garden back to them even if they offered me ten times the original asking price. I never enjoyed such privacy, such privacy and peace before, ever!

My neighbour must have burnt off some stubble and the smoke, still present in this early morning hour, triggers a memory of barbeque fires, blazing, smelly machines placed at the end of the neighbouring palisade fencing, just over the other side of my English garden. It started at 11:00 in the morning and it continued till late in the evening. Initially it was only at weekends, then gradually every day of the summer holidays. Our windows firmly shut to keep out the offensive odours, our only refuge the parks of the nearby National Trust property. Back at night, when we were returning home, the belching, smouldering monsters, giving off the stench of oily, greasy, charred bones as if from an arson of caged animals, were hiding from sight, ready to pounce again with claws of steel, teeth of coal and seething of greasy jaws. On approaching the fence, I could feel their wet, flaring nostrils hissing with rage as their tamers poured soapy solutions on them to clear any evidence of murderous deeds. But this gentle burning of straw and pruned branches is sublime by comparison; it reminds me of roasted chestnuts on an open fire, one late autumn afternoon. How soothing and restorative a scent. Retrospectively, I never really enjoyed my English garden, too smelly in the summer with the heat, too cold and often windy for the remaining part of the year, and only just glimpsed from indoors in between hospital shifts through the kitchen windows. Yes, I still think of it with longing and affection. Well, we say that distance makes the heart grow fonder; how very true. Besides, one tends to miss something or someone in spite of previous neglect or having been hardly acquainted, when it is time to say goodbye. In fact we never fully appreciate what we have till we lose it by any means. Then all merits and positive aspects cast a rosy glow on the negative traits that use to annoy us. I have learnt the hard way to enjoy what I have and appreciate the good qualities now rather when it is too late. Maybe for that very reason, I am here this morning, waiting for my guests, to welcome them and to offer them my eternal friendship as a token of true gratitude for their, maybe off the cuff, gesture? I intend this garden to remain a secret, as in visited only by people I approve of. Yes, I need a place of my own to be myself, the only way it may fit me for the day, in total abandon and deliverance from the artifices of modern life. Because what is freedom if not the possibility to allow whom I respect to just be? Take slugs and snails for instance, I chose toxic, drought-resistant and drought-loving perennial climbers and other plants to prevent the gastropods from feasting on them. On the other hand, plenty of native vegetation such as the Primula vulgaris abound alongside the perimeter of the lawn along with strawberries and sorrel, real delicacies for our friends. Everything must be allowed to live in harmony and when respected, Nature loves you back. I enjoy large garden snails and Roman snails (*Helix pomatia*) so much so that I am creating my own replicas as artifacts which I seed around the garden, through the cracks of the syenite blocks and other strategic corners. Their foot is made of stone I find on my walks down the hill, either slightly tapered or fluted at one end with a bulge at the other end and a flat base that they may be gently raised from the ground, too. And the shells are real ones, discarded by the deceased animals and gathered from the garden at the foot of the dry-stone walls. These mortal coils of expired animals are then washed and varnished with clear nail polish to give them a shiny lust. The tentacles, twigs from fallen branches, the whole composition sealed in place with hot glue. To the untrained eye, these decoys look very real. A real menace to the local birds, in fact, who look for soft morsels to satisfy their appetite. Crows are particularly partial to snails. Suffice to say three weeks ago, I was counting my fake snails, when I noticed the one next to the looking glass was not its usual self. On closer inspection I realized the shell had been broken or better smashed in several places, still maintaining its outlining shape. It resembled many shells I came across in the countryside which had been broken into by means of a pointed object in order to extract the soft animal inside. That is the work of crows, whom I witnessed flying at a certain height over a tarmacked road and drop a snail on it in order to crack the shell. My fake snail was still in place with its twiggy tentacles and stony foot intact. I could only deduce that a bird used its powerful beak to smash the shell. What a surprise when it realized the anticipated soft, chewy foot was the consistency of its own beak. Crows are said to be very intelligent birds, so from now on I will not expect any more accidents with my fake snails. Surely they will be respected aforehand!

I am sure my guests will love them and they may even point out that in fact I have too many snails crawling around before understanding their origin. Tiny objects lurking within hidden niches and behind more evident features, have always attracted my attention first as opposed to larger ones. I suppose it has to do with my propensity to promote attention to detail. I wonder which of the focal points my guests will notice first, Prometheus, the Roman amphora, or the french windows into the neighbouring lawn? I guess it largely depends on their tastes and inclinations. The three points are placed around a horseshoe area at different heights and are all appealing in their own way.

'Focal points are an essential feature of every garden, large or small, aspiring to success', reads one of my gardening magazines. I collected quite a few second-hand plants and gardening books along with buying monthly issues of gardening magazines which deal with green outdoor sowing, growing, bedecking and designing your own space. I absorbed the suggestions, advice, knacks, must do and must have with voracious interest, pretending I already had a green capacity to play with. Yes, if you wish a dream to come true you must project your hopes into a virtual reality and think and act as if it were already existing. So I did and last summer I lived in a parallel world of flowery borders, fragrant bushes and curtains of be-jewelled climbers of all hues and shapes. The grass on the lawn felt like a carpet of velvet under my bare feet and, before I knew it my fictitious garden started taking root inside me, establishing itself, nourished by my love, passion and belief in the power of achievement.

'Good things come to those who wait', I kept repeating to myself and so I started tending my imaginary garden ready to transfer my newly acquired green-fingers-know-how to the real thing when, not if, it materialized. Amongst all the information from the rich gardening literature I indulged in on a daily basis, the 'focal points' business, as in points of immediate attraction to the eyes of a visitor, caught my artistry and my mind began to conjure up all sorts of tricks to make my virtual and future garden a starting point of interesting conversation besides conveying a feeling of an aesthetically beautiful place while I would be in my garden to enjoy it. 'Something must catch a visitor's awareness' I told myself, as soon as someone steps over the gate threshold. And there, on top of the red brick, one hundred and fifty seven centimetres tall column, on its syenite capital, a thirty centimetre tall, hollow head of what I interpret to be a Greek mythological figure; its forehead truncated longitudinally, midline, to accommodate a plant pot of my choice. Yes, this imposing character, is in fact an attractive cement head planter. The facial features sport a straight, long nose, severe eyes, fleshy lips and a mane of thick, curly hair cascading from the temple region of the head to join an equally thick and wavy beard. I could think of one beloved figure from the past, Prometheus. Its looks gravely and judgingly meet the newcomers' eye with a clear admonition demanding decorum and respect for this Titan and supreme trickster. A fore-thinker par-excellence and crafty counsellor who moulded mankind out of clay, is here translated in his leading wish to mould the novitiate's behaviour into the realm he was called upon to guard from the top of the column. The legend goes that Prometheus stole wisdom form Athena and fire from Ephestus, which he donated to the human race whom he also taught the sciences and arts besides gifting it with hope, a virtue mankind can revert to in the face of misfortune. Prometheus is definitely my sort of guy and what better hair do could match its naturally thick crimp than a prostrating Sedum seboldii medio variegatum whose round succulent leaves filter the rays of the sun with a rich golden, orange and copper hue? It looks down on everyone entering the garden like a god does, from the top of Mount Olympus. This ancient, mediterranean presence conveys a classic appearance to my hidden paradise and sets the theme for the second focal point which stands tall at one hundred and fifty centimetres, and ruddy, two feet from the south-western corner of the garden.

"Wow, look what I found under the staircase!" I remember uttering in complete amazement while exploring nooks and crannies of our Italian house which was being renovated from top to bottom. My husband had to help me to gently rotate its base out of its well-concealed space and, when it eventually surfaced unscathed, I was confronted with a terracotta amphora in the style of ancient Roman pottery design. Clearly a garden feature which got damaged in the past as half its body, broken, had been stuck back together with a special resin. Two angular side handles in the neck region and an assortment of decorative carvings around the entire body, captured my fancy and was stood in the corner of the garden, on top of four cotto tiles which we retrieved from the original plot rubbish mound which contained, amongst other things, some intact terracotta, square tiles. The amphora elongated, capacious body could not be utilized as a planter, unless I sealed the neck two thirds down with an impermeable material (aluminium foil) and inserted a pot which got stuck just above the foil. Few days later I found just what I needed and purchased the correct sized pot containing Alyssum saxatile and Iberis umbellata bedecked with sprays of English variegated Ivy. I am now in love with the result and with Prometheus's gaze of approval, its multicoloured mop waving audaciously, in a puff of wind. But, I thought, it was not complete. One amphora was not enough however imposing and beautiful it might be, its surroundings were bare and wanting. I had to push myself further, to create a lavish appearance of this once meaningless corner which used to house the sludgy tubs, towered by a young Bay laurel tree. The latter now proudly boughs over the planted amphora as if to oblige with much needed shade. In fact this is a very humid area where moss and snails have taken up abode. Now, when building the climbers support made of poles and netting, three poles were left over, two hundred and five metres long of heavy metal, varnished green. What about standing them at an angle on three corners at the base of the amphora and converging their opposite ends above it? Just in the fashion of a purpose-made obelisk? So, they formed the perfect support for more creepers which I chose to be Lonicera (Honeysuckle) and Clematis needing plenty of moisture. Two months later, after planting, they are winding their way up the poles in a twisting, intermingling, gripping embrace with soft tendrils like the tentacles of an octopus. Needless to say, some new shoots are making their appearance, too and join the already intricate spiraling and entwining of the mother plant. What a scene! So appealing and totally transformational for the appearance of our amphora. This enigmatic amphora, how did it ever end up in my house in the first place, I wonder; but then, I do remember, it goes back to a good thirty years ago. My father, when he was still working as a building entrepreneur, had been commissioned by an industrialist to revamp his 18th century villa, standing on a hillock overlooking the provincial, winding road of our pre-Alpine valley surrounded by a large park on different terraced levels where ancient conifers, horse chestnut, beech and sequoia trees grew. As part of the main structural refurbishment, the owner was keen on making a clean breast of all furniture, in his view, no longer in keeping with the villa newly renovated style. The amphora was discovered below the house, under a portico of Corinthian design columns. It was leaning against the wall in two halves, of no longer any value, according to the owner, since broken beyond repair. My father made a beeline towards it and moved it into the courtyard with a pile of other junk. He was instructed to organize a pick-up truck for the disposal of the cast offs. As one would expect, before the arrival of the van, my father had loaded the two halves of the severed vase, along with other unsolicited items into his own van bound for his warehouse. The amphora was then repaired and stored under the staircase, undoubtedly lying there, forgotten for thirty odd years till my rediscovery upon inheriting the ancestral home, from my late father. No prior history is known; however, a search on a dedicated website, lists similar designs of terracotta amphoras as dating back to the 19th century, liberty style an Italian variant of Art Nouveau or Style Jules Verne (mainly associated with France) which flourished during the Belle Epoque, having an estimated worth of six hundred Euros. Not that I would put a monetary value on its origin, but it is, nevertheless, a very interesting and aesthetically engaging piece. So much so that in my puny garden it is one of the main focal points, conveying an elegant classic outlook to the overall garden appointment.

The clock tower chimes again the half hour past nine.

Time, inside the hidden garden, where contemplation and relaxation intermingle with past memories, takes up a completely different meaning. The local bells are operated by a clock work mechanism which plays melodic tunes at 05:00 and 06:00 o' clock in the afternoon and other special occasions and the motif of the notes may vary. The sound is enchanting and comes from just a few yards away, to travel in concentric bronze waves as far as the mouth of the valley, two kilometres away to then dissolve in a silver treble clef against the walls of the town. I can hear the chimes from home and they are like a call from my garden, to remind me of its constant pulsating, live presence, populated with animals and plants, thriving under the hospices of my Green Man. Now, I had the amphora with the floral top, the trellis with several climbers, but the spot called for more, still. I had to fill the space in front of the amphora and two terracotta, rectangular pots fitted the bill as they now looked like two long slippers worn by the ornament above. Lemon thyme and Thymus saturjoides my choice of fragrant herbs which with time will bend forward to form a carpet on the tiles. I observe this very effective composition and I remember it only took me one week to assemble it with items which were already in my possession. However, the whole vision for the project occurred in a couple of hours. Is it my creativity alone or the influence of the gardening magazines? Well, both, because I noticed that magazines suggest the trend of the moment proposing expensive alternatives and designs dictated by fashion. My moves are dictated by need and frugality and what I read and see can be used as a pointer towards more simple but equally accomplished solutions. My seventy odd square metres space speaks volumes with little money, second-hand items and my inventiveness. Only a few suggestions from the magazines were taken on board, and the points of convergence for attention were definitely something that before then had not naturally entered my mind. I look through the north-facing wall and over its entrance consisting of a sixty one by forty six centimetres aperture that allows me to enjoy the open extension to my garden. I never thought my little plot could look and feel so spacious. There is a little mini Pinscher wagging its tail at me in the far distance, whose dog is it? I have mine next to me and that leads to the third centre of attention. Two tall mirrors placed side by side stuck under the moss covered, tiled roof of the granite wall. The wall separates my property from my neighbour's which is one and a half metres lower than mine on the other side. These two mirrors reflect my lawn and the south-facing wall with the planted border and the creepers on a trellis system, conveying the illusion of a large french window opening out into the neighbour's property which for some bizarre reason is an identical copy of my rambling Honeysuckles, pannicles of yellow Thapsus, large bushes of Lavender and Sage and the waxy rosettes of the green Echeveria sporting leaning, long and velvety stems bearing pink and yellow florettes. As one strolls either the west-facing or east-facing walls one can catch a glimpse of an ever-changing realm beyond the window in the stone enclosure, as beguiling features appear and disappear with each step. This must be the highlight of the entire garden display. The mirrors have been angled in such a way as to reflect the environment opposite and sideways, giving an one- hundred-and-eighty-degree view of the garden as the visitor gently strolls along, on the terracotta tiles marking the pathway that runs alongside the perimeter that delimits both the borders and the lawn edges. In fact the illusion is so well accomplished the garden has become twice its original size. I just wonder whether Alice in the Wonderland, finding herself one summer evening skip- hopping around my garden, would have gone through my fake window in the wall, to find herself in a fantastical world of illusion. I do not need to be Alice, because just as I peek into my looking glass my creative power transports me into a wonderful world beyond this hidden garden conveying a sensation of deep, happy emotions which overwhelm me just as they did when, as a child, I used to frequent and hide in the woodland, on the *outskirts of my village to feel the encompassing embrace of Nature. Once I realized the mirrors optical illusion was successful, it was imperative to add some details and components that notably expanded the fake vision through the artificial opening. Two small, wrought iron trellis, one against one mirror, the other positioned at an acute angle so as to mimic an half open gate before the second mirror, added a touch of tangible reality. Then a trailing vine of fake Ivy with large leaves was strung across the top and along the sides of each mirror to create the impression of true Ivy branching out from a network of the living specimen creeping on the stone wall. At the foot of the mirrors, three medium sized, seasoned terracotta tiles provided the ideal step through the mystical gateway. A Dryopterix long-fronded fern was planted by one side of the mirror with the closed gate, so that its double by the reflection, added depth to the garden beyond. I included bark chips by scattering them around the flagstones to prevent any mud from spattering on the mirrors on rainy days. What was still missing were some lamps to guard and light up the gateway. Two solar-powered carriage lanterns took stand one on each side to the entrance through the wall. I admire my design and cannot prevent myself from commending my artistic gardening vision. Yes, I can see the fern fronds stroking the looking glass, ferns, these archetypal* specimens of prehistoric origin unchanged by the millenia, hold a captivating attraction. According to popular folklore, ferns are symbolic of security, love, and confidence besides everlasting youth. The last characteristic bodes well for my entire garden collection since a youthful look through the act of rebirth and renovation promoted by the presence of my Genius Loci, is a wish-come-true and very welcomed, indeed. In my mind's eye, the Dryopterix placed by the looking glass evokes the image of a primeval custodian of a magical gate from the present into the past and back into the present. It is a flashback into our human origin, of how we came to be on Earth and how far we have come as a species. However, the ferns serve as a warning from our destructive nature and often unrestricted power because we are no Dryopterix capable of evolutionary survival through the epochs; if we carry on along our path of annihilation we may disappear as a race, while the ferns will cover the planet making use of the nutrients from our decomposing bodies. My guests are surely going to be impressed and I shall savour the moment they discover my magical door is but a figment of their imagination. The door is set in what they used to know as the continuous wall made of uneven syenite blocks whose cracks and fissures were filled with quick-setting, coarse cement. Will they feel cheated? Pleasantly surprised, left wanting to know more or will they laugh out aloud at my failed attempt to trick them into believing there is a world beyond a world that lies hidden behind a shrouded, green, iron gate? While conjuring up all sorts of possible outcomes from my guests' visit, my eyes are attracted by a crimson Parrot tulip above the fence, on top of the wall, I never noticed before. Suddenly, the crested chalice emits a raucous crow which stands me at attention, while the hens coo, peck, lay eggs, and frantically scratch the ground in search of worms. The cockerel cocks its head to one side and throws me a curious look. What am I doing sitting at a table under the sunshade staring at him? Where do I come from? Up to one year ago, this space housed a patch of tall, wild grasses where the neighbouring cats used to lie and stretch in the lazy afternoon sun. Its jady eye darts up and down taking in the transformation and, after a construed pose he opens his beak, tosses his blazing, fleshy crest, stretches his neck heavenward and launches a high-pitched call, 'cock-a- doodle-doooo' as if in approval of the improvement down below its bare roost. Then he disappears back into his coop. I am glad even the neighbour's king of the lodge displays and vocally demonstrates some artistic interest beyond his immediate household affairs. In fact a gardener's appointments with their thoughtful arrangements around the available constrained space, is but pure aesthetic prowess which complements the living world made of adaptive plants, invertebrates and insect life. While admiring my amphora I can't help capturing the presence of a much smaller, yet impressive, secondary focal point which I positioned at the foot of the Bay laurel tree, in its shady and wet area, a few centimetres behind the amphora, to its right as you enter the garden. It is a terracotta head of a cherub, lips pursed, eyes closed as if savouring a special moment, in a 'sniffing the morning air' position, to be bottled and preserved for eternity. The two terracotta objects, although totally different, have the same colour and the cherub's head serves the purpose to enhance the perspective at the point where the south and west walls meet. Besides, the addition of a small mirror leant against the wall at the appropriate angle, behind some cropped grass, offers a glimpse of the valley through the wall by reflecting the lower branches of the pear tree and a slice of sky above. The visitors are invited to take a peek through the small aperture, curious of what may lie beyond since the mirror cleverly avoids their own reflection. Around the base of the cherub's neck, a garland of red-dotted Drosanthemum in bloom, replicates an emerald necklace bearing interspersed rubies to indicate the cherub's noble origin.

 A puff of breeze billows the curtains hanging from the entrance gate and I turn around startled lest someone is trying to force their entry through my unlocked gate. One quick look reassures me that the key in the lock is firmly turned and my visitors will have to announce their presence before coming in. My extensive reading made clear that amongst the statuary and miscellanea ornaments of an outstanding garden, especially so if it displays a classic character, is the presence of a fountain. Be it made of cement or terracotta or metal, even plastic would do. Water is essential to a garden as blood is essential to us. 'Even drought-loving plants need a splash ever so often'. That statement worried me no end, because there is no running water in my garden as previously mentioned. However, this day and age there is no surrendering to any difficulties, any obstacle is a challenge to be met and the perceived problem to be overcome with skill and inventiveness. A quick search landed me in the right place, a solar-powered disk with a spout in the middle onto which a number of different disgorging adaptors can be fitted to produce a sparkling fountain with multiple jets. All that it required was to initially charge up the self-recharging battery and then plunge the disk into the water, taking care that the spout was above the water level. I could only afford a tall, fake, terracotta fountain made up of a pedestal and a round basin which could serve the dual purpose of a fountain and a bird bath. Once I had assembled the fountain, filled it with two thirds of clean water and lowered the disk into it, the effect was spectacular. A jet of water sprang upwards forming an unbrella-shaped shower, before falling back into the basin. The pump kept re-circulating the water which glistened with hundreds of golden and silver droplets, like jewels glittering in the sun. The splashing sound of the drops that bounced back onto the bath and the fine trickling that brought the fountain to life were extremely soothing, a quintessential feature of my garden for most part of the year. The fountain is now playing delicately, its silvery fingers percussing its imaginary xilophone along with the gentle notes of a fluty breeze, amongst the Robinia trees leaves. It is one of the most enjoyable of musical duets I have been entertained by and it goes on all day long to cradle my dreams and stroke my heart. The fountain is a mobile feature and it can be positioned anywhere in the garden. For the moment it stands diagonally a few steps away from Prometheus near the corner where the western wall meets the northern one, and just there, nestled amongst the Ivy trails, sits an amber glass insect reading a book. This very beautiful ant holding a solar light inside its transparent abdomen was a gift from a friend who thought an insect-lover like me would appreciate the charm of such an unique object to add some mystery, in amongst the foliage, on a summer night. She was spot on. The ant has been growing some succulent plants around itself, a Sedum sieboldii which, along with the Ivy sprays, *provide some much needed shelter from the unwanted claws of some impulsive bird of prey. And my fountain continues its cheerful tune, singing in the sun, in the wind and only stops when the sun sets behind the curve of the mountain or moves behind the canopies of the tall trees. It starts by slowing down, its spray half its usual height, hiccupping as the foliage above, shaken by the breeze cover and uncover the radiance behind them, in a shower of glittering shards of light. Then, as the hot disk disappears below the horizon, the fountain produces a few coughs and a final splatter, like the exhausts of a car that has seen better days and chokes in its own smoky emissions. Then suddenly nothing more can be heard and the long shadows of the trees run across the lawn, like giant, spectral limbs resurrected from their boles that kept them concealed in the day time world. I am perturbed remembering the beautiful fading of my fountain, at the incipient falling of dusk, so sudden, so unexpected. How to go about it in the absence of piped water? Then, an idea strikes me; a looking glass, yes, a looking glass, not on the wall but interred and protected by a transparent cover to reflect the sky. That could be another trick to fake a pond. Yes, a pond! What an idea! All I had to do was to sit anywhere in the garden, observe the immediate area around me, and unleash my creativity. The imitation pond will be a permanent feature to shift my attention to when, as* daylight starts fading away, my solar fountains inevitably fails to sing. And that is the feature I placed by the amphora, at the foot of its terracotta tiles. I employed a transparent, plastic aquarium, sank it into a rectangular hole, as deep as the size of the container itself, to ensure its brim was level with the ground around it. I then stuck some self-adhesive mirror sheets onto the bottom and added some stones I had collected from the stream. I sealed the box with a transparent sheet of perspex which, according to the temperature and weather conditions, either steams up or collects droplets on its internal surface, thus mimicking the foam or spray drops of a bubbly spring. As the mirror reflects the sky, the illusion of water can either be blue or murky still showing the additional feature of some sailing clouds, on occasion. The inclusion of a few strands of false, green algae by the edges of the pond conveys the semblance of movement, of deeper water currents sweeping past the algae, perpetually. Around the pond I placed round pebbles of different sizes to mimic the effect of a rocky shore. In between the stones, I placed miniature pots containing succulents and some of my stone and shell snail crafts. It is satisfactory enough to be an artist, but beauty is in the eye of the beholder and for this very reason I cannot wait to hear the opinions of my to-be-visitors. What I love the most in my garden is the corner where the hole in the wall, the cherub head, the giant amphora and the fake pond with the scented trailing Thyme behind it, all come together harmoniously, adding remoteness and graded perspective; a veritable diversion from what used to be the darkest (below the Bay laurel tree and under the hanging neighbouring pear trees heavy fronds) and dullest of spots in the original plot. Any visitor can become fully engaged and engrossed in being met with the immediate focal points of the mobile fountain, the scrutinizing eyes of Prometheus, the five features corner, starring the amphora, and next to them the magic looking glass. Of course, any gardener can tell you that in order to preserve your lawn you must lay down a path. As I follow the movement of the one I set down, I can never guess that only three months ago it did not exist. A snaky terracotta path made of moss-stained, square tiles in single file, at a distance of approximately twenty centimetres from one another, leads the way along the borders and up to each centre of attention which, after the initial visual impact on entering the garden, call for a closer inspection for the full appreciation of the maverick mind behind the well-crafted illusions. By all means, I am no expert and this is my very first attempt at designing, planting and furnishing a garden of my own. Modesty apart, it looks, feels, sounds and smells pretty impressive and I am thoroughly pleased with the outcome. I am also quite excited (and so are my-to-be-visitors; one of them told me on the phone that over this past year, they have been wondering how their bare plot of native grasses and weeds had been turned around, after I had come to be in its possession, officially on the 4th of October 2022) to see my visitors' reaction. Initially I suggested we meet at their house so that I could show them my garden plan, the watercolours illustrating the various features; the type of plants I was proposing to buy, my daily gardening journal reporting lists of both accomplished and pending jobs, the materials used, the step-by-step development of what I can witness in the garden now, the aspects, the micro climatic soil properties, water and sun availability during the changing seasons, how extensive frost would be in the winter and what fauna I was to contend my space with. By modern terms, fauna is referred to as garden pests. However, as soon as I became the proprietor of the plot, I was adamant I had to enhance the Spirit of the Place represented by my crafted Green Man, resting within the corner found by the northern wall and the stone column that delimits the entrance to the garden. My philosophy is to open one's conscience to the voice of the universe within which Nature and its laws rest. I am a guest in this corner of the Earth and in order to be and feel welcomed I must respect the creatures who found their abode here before my arrival in order that the essence of the true ethos of the area is preserved as much as possible and we can all share the beauty and wisdom that comes with living in symbiosis with one another. When I started moving things around in the garden to create a specific space, corners, mounds from my plants, shrubs and trees I was mindful of causing a disturbance to the ground-dwellers. In fact, in the corner between the eastern and southern walls, I dismantled a pile of earth, rubble, debris, sherds, countless terracotta tiles and small and larger fragments of the same material, local stones, discarded snail shells, broken pottery and a rectangular tile dating back to the turn of the last century, even a glass marble, with green coils inside, to enjoy the kiss of the sun after, who knows how many decades, as it was buried really deep. Amongst the items, I found a fairly large and a smaller sherd of terracotta tile bearing the imprints of a small dog's paws. Where did the tiles come from in the first instance? They must be ancient, because only tiles left out to dry in an artisanal furnace can be exposed to the visit of a curious, wondering pet, who inadvertently walks all over the soft material before it can be set hard. Amongst all these curios (which I washed, brushed, dried and preserved) I discovered all sorts of creatures, which, as I proceeded with my work, scuttled left and right, terrified by the presence of this impolite and inconsiderate intruder. Centipedes, millipedes, earwigs, fat and glossy earthworms, woodlice, beetles of unknown species to me, slugs of different colours, garden snails and Roman snails, lay with their collection of white, moist and sticky eggs, they all tried to flee or withdraw inside their shells. I took great care in moving them to the wet areas of the plot and, afterwards, once I sifted through the large amount of terracotta tile sherds, I made a skirting board up against the perimeter of two walls, the southern and eastern one, by leaning the better sherds against the foot of the walls, their pointed ends uppermost, their flat ends gently pushed into the earth to add stability. The space behind the sherds thus created, dark, moist and cool, has been providing a safe, ideal haven for the friends I displaced, out of my own need. Now, on occasions, I lift the sherds away from the walls to reveal, even on such scorching days during the heat waves, that have plagued our normally fresh climate, all sorts of invertebrates dwelling happily in their purpose-made abodes which I am proud to say worked to perfection. The same goes for some native plants or wind-seeded ones which determine the green character of the plot. In between the cracks of the stone-walls which are built with irregularly dressed, rectangular syenite blocks, Greater celandine, Mint, Potentilla indaca, various species of moss; Kenilworth Ivy (also known as Cymbalaria muralis), Maidenhair (Spleenwort) thrive, drawing their nutrients from the scarce *particles of soil carried by the wind and the dust that deposit themselves on the crumbling, old cement used to fill the gaps in the past, by utilizing the heat of the sun, much stronger because absorbed by the stone and radiated back to the environment at dusk and last but not least, the rain water. These plants high resistance to drought means they do not need to be artificially watered; the exception is the Cymbalaria, which swings in the breeze, a mere brownish, long and uncouth beard over prolonged rain-less periods, makes a surprising and unexpected come back when the moist conditions return. Just two stones are enough to induce its winking blue eyes to open through its delicate green curtains of heart-shaped leaves. All this and more I was proposing to discuss with my guests prior to their visit but the element of surprise could not be spoilt with advance information. They have a mental image of what their plot looked like when they sold it to me. Now I'd like to wow them out of their wits by the stark and amazing transformation I was able to achieve with no prior knowledge or experience in the field of gardening. I want to fuel their curiosity as to how, what, when, who, with what, why and how come I have obtained such results in a relatively short space of time. The questions the garden will elicit will then take me back to the drawing board so I can explain, highlight and show them what I aspired to and, will* they honestly tell me whether I have achieved my aim; if not, what has fallen short of my expectations and, whether I have exceeded my goal and hopes. Will they care to share their impressions with me? I must admit that, for a rather bizarre reason, I feel responsible towards this garden which, although legally mine, still belongs in spirit, partially to my guests. I have this profound feeling of togetherness with these people I truly hardly know at all but whom I am becoming very close to through this garden, in fact it is the garden that has brought us together. Incredible to think this way, but true. I was desperately looking for a green land to love and they had been looking for someone to love and cherish the land they had tried to sell in vain, simply because they instinctively knew how to distinguish a genuinely caring person from a superficial one. Destiny brought us together, literally in a matter of seconds. It is really spooky and even now, within these four walls while waiting for these special people after a whole year since we briefly met, I perceive a benevolent, relaxing aura around me, as if I were about to welcome back some long-lost, old friends who decided to bequeath this garden on me as a token of their faithfulness over the years. This is a very significant and extraordinary situation; a unique opportunity to partake in the gift of love. Some of the objects I found in the mound of rubble and earth, I have displayed around the Green Man, safely under his sealed bell jar; the large terracotta tile with several paw prints I have placed under a transparent plastic cover, moderately interred around its edges, on the south-facing border. It gives the impression of being an ancient Roman pottery find, and a fine archeological piece to exhibit or even flaunt in my garden. As I scan the western fence I lay my eyes on a fairly large, stoppered glass jar, normally used for keeping sweets. It rests on its side, slightly inclined so as not to be completely flat. It is now the 'glass jar of my garden secrets'. As time goes by, I shall deposit small, folded sheets of paper disclosing the whereabouts of some hidden treasures, inside it. They will be useful both as a reminder to me and as a possible game for visitors. They will be invited to look for the objects I have hidden around the garden, to add to its secret charm. Fast developing foliage can easily conceal my little artifacts for good and if even moss creeps over them, they would disappear from sight and from my mind altogether. Originally I bought the jar for a completely different purpose. I had filled it with spring water in which I had immersed a rich variety of wild flowers I had picked in the evening of Saint John, on June 23rd. The legend goes that when a bowl of spring water in which a variety of wild, summer flowers are floated, is left out to catch the night dew, the water becomes imbued with magic powers because the dew is thought to fall from Heaven.

On the morning of the 24th, we should rinse our faces and hands with the afore-prepared floral water in order to propitiate a vigorous, healthy and abundant summer season. True to the folklore I did rinse both face and hands with the mystical water the morning after preparing it. Subsequently, I emptied the contents of the jar in a corner of the garden to harness in the energy of the universe in my square of Eden. However, one detail that truly stunned me was one photo (out of the several ones I had taken of the floral jar standing on the lawn) which showed an opalescent, wide shaft of sunshine hitting the jar obliquely as one witnesses in the depiction of divine intervention, in the shape of a brilliant ray of silvery-golden light. Could the uncanny enchantment really strike? Aside from the magical aspect, the water was fresh and exuded a melange of sweet scents that were extremely pleasant to the senses.

A strong puff of wind lifts the brim of the tilted parasol and the foliage of the hangers dance disorderly exchanging arms and sliding past one another with mounting vitality, as the tapering boughs creek, wailing and groaning under the wait of their green and yellowing, nuanced apparel. Black, rolling clouds, frothing at the edges, are building up in the north, their appearance similar to a flock of Herdwick sheep, sweeping down a mountain slope. As the air current gains strength, the disheveled front combines and divides into monstrous shapes with bulgy, weeping eyes, the presage of a deluge of torrential rain about to break out. Then, no sooner had the adverse weather front emerged than it started to be broken up like grease fleeces in the expert hands of a professional wool sorter. Now, the bank of white and grey fluff is quickly dismantling, a few streaks of smoke being dispersed beyond the horizon. Everything calms down and the canopies above, slowly breathe gentle sighs of relief in the soft intermittent zephir. We are in the grip of a ferocious heat wave for the second time this year. Gone are the halcyon days of balmy and dreamy summer times when the earth absorbed the sunshine at day time to radiate it back at dusk, gifting all living creatures with pleasantly warm, heavily scented breezes, alive with the notes of serenading crickets; evenings and nights feeling like velvet, the vault above winking with silver stars intermingled with the erratic golden-green lights of the fireflies' lanterns. Now, the extreme temperatures have shortened the natural world nuptuals and by as early as mid-June both crickets and grasshoppers are already quiet in their baked tombs of earth. All fledgelings have taken to their wings and the canopies of some trees which only one month before were unfurling the upper page of their leaves eagerly seeking the kiss of the sun, are already heralding a precocious autumnal season with golden and crimson locks showing through their green manes. A lot of them, too many indeed, stretch their spectral hands sideways and upwards, shaking and gesticulating horribly, perhaps in an attempt to find help, their flesh mercilessly and gradually being destroyed in an agonising feasting ritual at the mercy of the invading Popilia Japonica. I remember my first encounter with these, I'd say quite strikingly beautiful beetles with rigid elytra of shiny, metallic green and bronze diodes being reflected on and off depending on the viewing angle; their characteristic five patches of white hairs on each side of the abdomen and two more on the upper side of the last abdominal segment. The pronotum and head are invariably jade green and metallic in their appearance. I was so taken by their beauty I drew and painted in watercolour an A3 portrait of one of these amazing specimens. I later found out about its veracity and how colonies of them sit on trees and certain plants unleashing their voracious appetite which result in their meal leftovers as the mid rib and veins or the skeletonized version of a former leaf. A similar beetle, the Rose chafer (Cetonia aurata) lacks the tufts of white hairs but it is indigenous and more readily kept under control. I was fooled by the iridescence of their bodies and only now I have learnt the difference. I was spurred into action to save my garden from a potential Popilia invasion when, a few weeks ago I spotted whole branches of skeletonized leaves quivering on the plum tree belonging to my neighbours, whose gnarled, extended boughs reach over the south-west corner of my garden.

No specimen could be detected on any of my plants and a quick search landed me with a solution of Neen oil whose smell keeps the Japonica at bay. All my plants have now been sprayed on including my neighbours' lower and overhanging pear and plum trees branches. Thank God for the internet. Amongst all the rubbish one may come across (with the use of a facility which is now marred with so called fake and unfounded information) there is still scope for acquiring correct and useful information which one must carefully filter through a critically analysed framework of reference. It is a very complicated world the one we are living in nowadays, far too complex in fact for the average person to understand, or even bother to make sense of. That is why I believe the rise of artificial intelligence is inevitable. However, the simple ebbs and flows of the living creatures within my garden walls keep me in touch with Nature's universal intelligence and preserves mine. So, I am definitely grateful for the advice I found within the on-line literature, not only about the Popilia but also regarding drought-resistant or drought-loving plants. Had I simply chosen any plant for the beauty of their blossom, scent and overall appearance, I would have ended up with a dead garden scorched by the fierce and relentless heat of the summer sun. My initial desire was to create a room of living green walls dotted with blooms through the seasons; borders of evergreen succulents, bushes and perennial plants all displaying their inflorescences in a staggered fashion throughout the year with clusters of delicately tinted and scented blooms replaced by equally appealing and long-lasting berries, well into the winter months. Besides I have a proclivity for low maintenance, easy tending types of garden, which in my case was also dictated by the four aspects, the type of soil, the neighbouring overhanging trees and the shrubs, the weather and the lack of direct access to water and last but not least security, since my garden is situated back to back with a plot owned by my neighbour on the eastern aspect overlooking a wild and overgrown forest of briars proliferating over the western-looking fence, within my other neighbours' highly neglected property, the dark, hanging fronds of the pear and plum trees bent downwards even further in the autumn, under the weight of their ripening fruits on the southern aspect; and finally, a towering two metres tall wall of dry granite blocks separating my property from a public, cobbled path at the northern aspect of my garden. As far as the eastern and northern aspects were concerned a net-and- poles solution with appealing evergreen climbers, was a tall order for me. I remember searching for plants that can give you a permanent, fast coverage and the yellow Jasmine, Gelsemium sempervirens, comprising of five plants were thus staggered along their support in November. Back then they were one hundred and twenty centimetres tall, now they have exceeded two metres and are bushing up. I like the way they have been fingering their ascent through the soft, green netting frame after greeting me with a profusion of unequalled, golden, highly scented bells. Their tendrils are dangling over the netting looking for further support and some have inched their way across the net, crisscrossing one another filling every gap like a loom weaving a cloth with shiny, leafy threads. The threads spread wide and far like the web of a spider and once the living wall is complete, I will have reached my aim. Initially I was keen to ensure a tall wall to discourage the inquisitive looks of my otherwise discreet and kind neighbour, so I have no concern on that score. If I look northwards, the northern aspect sports a similar creeping support for different climbers. Three Trachelospermum jasminoides (the white, false Jasmine), one Passion flower plant; one Campsis (Madam Galen) in the middle, two Stephanotis jasmines and one Jasminum polyanthum by the entrance. Here my aim was to deter the neighbouring cats from jumping over the wall from the narrow alleyway, onto my wall (they are exceptionally good acrobats) and from there land onto my plot to find a suitable corner to relieve themselves, undisturbed both when we are not here and when they can hide themselves within the silent folds of the night. The results of my multiple planting is a second, thickly woven, green curtain dotted with white, caerulean and brilliant, deep orange inflorescences blooming at different times, some in unison. As I admire the outcome of my work, I cannot fail to spot an oval, green fruit dangling out of the sepals of a spent Passion flower bloom. It is the only one present at the moment amongst the thick network of fast-growing tendrils that hold a myriad of green blooms which open in turn, two or three at a time. At the foot of the netting lie two long and wide borders. These covered in conifer bark chips, have been planted with a rich variety of perennials, Sage, Lavender, Verbascum thapsus, Oxalis articulata, Campanulas and an Acacia mimosa, with a Planta genista against the stone pillar in the corner between the western and northern boundaries. The blend of scents from the mixture of plants which intensifies by a stroking hand or the caress of the wind is a special feature to me. Besides, an abundant insect life outnumbered by the threatened species of the Honey bee, constantly teem about my blooms attracted by the gentle perfume, in search of nectar. It is amazing how now I can just cast an eye around my own garden to see, smell and touch the plants that only one year ago were but photos in a gardening book or magazine whose only smell was that of a freshly printed, glossy page (for the magazines) and the rich weathered perfume exuding from yellowed pages of a bygone time, second hand, old book. Isn't it true that the Passion flower gets fertilized mainly by Honey bees and Carpenter bees? Well, in order to aid the process, I planted two Lavender bushes at each side of the Passion flower and they attract a good number of such bees throughout the day which can then make a small effort to buzz a little bit higher up to land the beautiful caerulean, crested blooms of my Passion flower plant. How come so far only one fruit has developed? The other flowers once faded, drop out leaving only one petiole attached to the tendril end? That is a mystery to me. Perhaps, later in the year I shall be pleasantly surprised to discover a few more round-bellied, fleshy pendants streaked with an orange, ripening glow.

At the foot of the southern wall, the aspect is humid, damp with the umbrage of the thick overhanging fruit trees provided by the gargantuan fall of the canopies in autumn which accumulates on the ground. This year, I shall regularly rake the lawn to prevent putrefaction and to ensure the upper level of the turf is adequately aerated and hence oxygenated. However, near the foot of the walls, a layer of cellulose will provide the organic material to feed into the soil and will shelter the hibernating creatures' sleep in winter. Having said that we have had milder winters over the past ten years and if the trend continues, more invertebrate animals will survive and will make an earlier come back in the spring. Here a rockery of ferns and a few resistant succulents along with the native Potentilla indica that by means of its adventitious rooting system spreads along the ground forming thick carpets of false strawberries from golden yellow flowers that ripen into upright red and round, bumpy fruity heads, are housed. More clumps of Oxalis love the moist conditions and open their magenta eyes to the touch of the morning sun, before the gentle dust of the evening, slowly, gracefully, lower their eyelids into their dusky green sepals. Everywhere, dotted around these three aspects of my garden, grow different species of semi-perennial succulent plants, all shape and sizes, bearing unthinkable names, Sempervivum tormentosum, Hens and chicks, Echeveria, Sedum sieboldii, Sempervivum tectorum rubi and Adromiscus diabolicus. Our friend, who after retiring, has been making ends meet by buying wood and then re-selling it to local customers who, for the majority have wood-burning stoves, commented on the fact I had labeled my plants:

"Don't you remember their names?", he asked in an off-the-cuff manner before reading some of the titles.

"Oh, all right, now I understand the presence of all these labels."

I grinned!

My succulents be-jewelled with green and red, bluish shades and variegated colours, the brown carpet of bark chips which on certain occasions, when baked by the sun, releases wafts of faintly scented resin. Some precious bushes such as Daphne odora and Nandina domestica share the space with Lemon beebrush, Melissa, upright Spanish lavender, pink and mauve, prostrated Rosemary, growing in a pot and my friend's gift, an Azalea plant. Truth to be told, even the combination of plants along with its external edging of medium size covered in moss, lends the illusionary look of a years' old mature garden, when in actual fact I chanced the choice of both vegetation and its positioning based uniquely on their height, tendency to spread and hardiness. I just planted and hoped for the best. Call it my luck or acquired skill but the result is astoundingly pleasing to all the senses and no one could have ever guessed that only five months ago this garden was but a bare plot of self-seeding grass, with some patches of wall crumbling; a mound of rubble and rubbish in one corner and two water tubs full of sludge material tucked underneath the trees canopies. No one, that is except for this morning's guests, previous owners of this property. However, even then it held that positive, mysterious charm that led me to formally purchase it.

"Hi, you are an early bird", called our newly made friend while we were walking the dog. "Are you visiting your garden?" he asked with a smile.

"Yes", I replied, "we spend both morning and afternoon there, almost every day".

"Well, cast an eye up there, on top of the dry-stone wall which runs along this road", he pointed out, "a friend told me to look after his little plot and should you be interested, he may sell it to you". After explaining it was too late for any purchase because we had already spent the money for acquiring our present garden, I followed him through a jaded, narrow and tall gate (just like mine was; I think it used to be a popular design of gate, wide enough to let a thin person through and recessed into the wall maybe to avoid attracting the attention of passersby to a private property) and a very steep, stone staircase (whose steps were so narrow as to warrant the safe ascent on tiptoes and the safe descent by laying down the ball of the foot alone, rather dodgy a practice and dangerous, too) which led to a wide grassed-over plot twice as big as mine bound on two sides by very tall walls; a few fruit trees with gnarled boles and branches inferred the past use of the area as an orchard.

What grabbed my attention and immediate interest was the back of the plot, well recessed under the trees and enjoying totally hidden privacy. However, my recent experience of having become the proud owner of Little HighGrove, highlighted some immediate drawbacks such as difficult accessibility up the narrow stone staircase, no running water and no access to it nearby; extreme difficulty in moving any material into the garden and, therefore, to plant borders, maintain them and to build a summer house. Should I still have been desperate for a green space of my own, I guess I would have been willing to compromise and to limit myself to mowing the lawn and to place a table and two chairs under the trees. As it stands, I was so lucky to meet the Carlone family and to come by a small, quaint square of beauty which now bears my mark of gardening, accomplished talent. I thought so much as ten minutes later I was turning the key into the lock of my property and, on opening the gate my eyes met with the outcome of my hard work, conveying a deep sense of joy and peace.

"Oilá", I start at the call behind my back. I know the tone of his voice. Amongst the woven curtains of yellow Jasmine, I can make out the round face and bold head of my neighbour who tries to raise his naked torso above the ensconcing climbers, his plump cheeks a full Moon rising fast from the concealed shape of a thickly forested hill.

"Hello", I reply without making an effort to seek to make eye contact.

"Enjoying the fresh summer morning?" he enquires.

"Yes, sure, I am waiting for some guests to visit".

"Oh, good, have a nice day, I'll see you next time", and in so saying his Moon face sets down as fast as it had risen leaving behind a blue sky effervescent with radiant sunlight.

I am so glad these over-the-fence encounters are few and far between, besides being brisk and all thanks to my tall climbers that afford me with a much sought after privacy and silence I could not be privy to anywhere else before. Talking about privacy, seclusion and safety, the western aspect of the garden, unlike the other three ones is not delimited by a wall but by a green metal fence tightly stretched in between four pillars in a row, two at the extreme corners made of syenite blocks and continuous with the southern and northern walls, respectively, and two in the middle, all equally spaced out from one another, made of red brick held together by cement and topped with a large, square syenite block as their capital, like the head cover of a British university student. The net sits on a row of syenite blocks placed horizontally along the perimeter of the lawn and are continuous with the dry-stone wall of my neighbours down below. The only suitable hedge to cover permanently this metal fence in order to keep off the disorderly bramble forest, is a Pyracantha hedge. The Pyracantha dense, white inflorescences, have now been replaced by clusters of green berries which will turn red and orange in the autumn, to last through the next spring. The advantage of these plants is the presence of five centimetres long, thin thorns distributed haphazardly along the entire length of each climbing branch. These plants grow (aided by careful pruning) into thick and deadly bushes in a relatively short time thus providing an impenetrable barrier to any would-be intruder. For the moment I have trained only the mother plant original branches across the fence in a fan-like fashion while I am waiting for the several side twigs to grow taller and to start adding volume to the hedge design. Before each thick column I planted a wild Cherry, now one metre taller than it was a month ago and a Spindle tree, the latter not so well developed yet but looking healthy. Now, since I have uprooted these two trees from the side of the wooded hill down below the garden, I cannot tell which type of wild cherry it is, although I suspect it may well be our native Prunus avium or sweet Cherry which bears small, red or burgundy fruit which in some cases have a slightly sour or bitter after taste but very flavourful, nevertheless. The beauty of the unknown is in the surprise of discovery; maybe, as soon as next spring/summer, once the organza petals have fallen, the shiny red fruits will make their mark into the world and only then, I'll be able to identify the species the tree belongs to. Of course a Cherry tree was a must have in my garden collection and I hope I never again have to say goodbye to this one as I had to do with my beloved English one. A dull 'thump' sound shakes me out of my thoughts and immediately attracts the attention of our mini Pinscher who springs on all fours and begins to bark madly at the would-be-intruder. It is one of the neighbouring cats who, by now, knows better than climbing on to the top of the wall trying a kamikaze descent with a view to dropping one of his renowned express parcels. Rosco jumps up and down while following the cat which darts along the wall and into the next door plot. Aside from natural plant remedies, I had to resort to a more artifitious human-devised cat repellent, duly cemented in place on top of the stone column capital flanking the right side of the entry gate.

"You would not have any dark glass, empty bottles, cousin, would you?" I enquired of my relative last year. His daughter arrived with a trug carrying a dozen empty wine bottles, although she could not, for the life of her, understand the reasons why I declined to have the relative bottles stoppers. It only took one bottle and one minute of my time to smash it inside a plastic bag with a hammer, to provide me with extremely sharp human and cat deterrents. The sherds cannot be viewed from the public way but could be *felt and seen with a sudden gush of red fluid and maybe a twinge of pain should anyone, carried too far by either their greed or unrestrained curiosity, attempt the climbing of the stone column to trespass into my square of paradise. I have noticed that this type of commonly built dry-stone walls made of block of syenite, all bear sherds of glass along the top aspect of their perimeter; a sure way to persuade any thug to keep to public soil only.*

The Martins which had been swooping and wheeling next to the ground, threatened by the rumbling of a potential storm, have now soared back into the blue depth of the firmament, gliding concentrically, darting in all directions at a drop of a hat, when some juicy beetles try some high flying manoeuvre into chartered, bird (avian) aerial territory.

The noise of people labouring in the valley down below is reflected back into the hill face, and, even without leaving my garden chair, I know Piera's son is mowing the family lawn, or the local farmer is turning the rows of hay bundles with his combined tractor.

Now, out of the blue Rosco, the nano Pinscher, is back in action while launching himself against the gate and, like a fury, teeth bearing down through curled upper lips, jaws shark-like, he has sniffed the presence of a dog walking past our gate; the latter hesitates a moment before engaging into a deadly jaw-breaking battle with the iron bars of our gate in an attempt to show his supremacy to Rosco. The owner calls and pulls her dog away. Rosco, convinced it is his "min-Pin's" invincible stance and aggression to have scared the contender away, cocks his leg against the curtain that hangs at the gate, then kicks the ground with his hind legs, gives himself a good scroll and, still mumbling to himself, trots to the water bowl in need of a thirst-quenching drink after his heart-racing, eye-bulging quarrel. He is a guard dog after all, in spite of his diminutive size. How this little dog with a larger-than-life personality came to be with us is extraordinary. Call it serendipity or a twist of fate! For over thirty years I had been yearning for a little dog, but my situation in England was against my wish. However, as soon as I came back to stay in Italy, two round, wet and black eyes as ripe as summer cherries, set into a diminutive black and auburn face, topped with an equally dark and wet nose, ears pointing upwards, had his little paws stuck to the neighbour's gate with a fast wind-screen wiper of a tail.

"Could I take him for a walk, please?" I asked Renata, Rosco's owner.

She has been my neighbour in the courtyard for over forty five years and she and her husband are getting on in their years, unfortunately, not in very good health.

"Yes, that would help because I can hardly stand on my feet these days and I seldom take him out. He was a gift, a rescue puppy from my son, two years ago. Meanwhile my health has been deteriorating and, alas, the dog, a nano Pinscher, is pretty always indoors."

Ever since that day, four years now, come rain or shine, Rosco is with us from 07:30 in the morning till 18:00 in the evening, sometimes even 20:00 hours. We have become his extended family and my husband and I are Uncle and Auntie to him. He has made plenty of four-legged friends during his daily walks and enjoys car trips aside from English and watercolour lessons. We are now inseparable!

Peace and quiet restored, I can sink back into my chair and, as I scan my garden with the eye of a doting mother, through the long, weeping fronds of the Dryopteris fern, I discern a cloaked, grey figure, shrouded in mystery and partly concealed in the dappled shade by the magic looking-glass. To the layperson he is but a grey, old man, covered in sweeping clothes, only showing his face, hands and sandled feet. He holds a spade with his right hand and pushes it into the soil with his right foot. On to his left arm a trug-bucket carrying a green plant and a garland of large flowers bedecking his left wrist. He is my Patron Saint, yes, the Patron Saint of gardeners' the world over, Saint Fiacre. The resin statue arrived only three days ago from Britain and its spirit hovering in the garden, will look after my efforts, dreams and well-being since I have had some back-breaking experiences in the making of my green paradise. Both Saint Fiacre and the Green Man are facing each other from opposite corners of the garden with their super powers of conservation and regeneration and cosmic goodness. They, together, promote the safekeeping of my garden as a complex living being, made up of many lives within and of my life and health as the human custodian responsible for the care of the life inside these boundaries and for the up-keeping of the garden's ancient walls. Earlier in my project I decided that with the auspices of the Spirit of the Place I would promote the symbiotic living of plants and the creatures who already inhabited the ground. The pinnacle of my success is shown by the outcome of the gardening toil, in the intact state of the leaves, the lusciousness of all plants along with the presence of gastropods, insects, invertebrates of the earth, pollinators and birds. It is as if the two presences in my garden whipped up a magnetic field within which everything vibrates at a higher frequency, pulsating and growing at remarkable speed. Also my wish for rain has been granted several times this year, contrary to the initial forecast. The whole of southern Europe has been experiencing temperatures normally found in the African continent. Here, however, only a few days of extreme heat were suddenly met with cooler air, well below the seasonal average, which resulted in copious amounts of rain throughout the spring and summer. I am glad to report that the cats that regularly used to litter the ground have almost disappeared from the garden. Any idea I implemented has paid off and it has even added to the charm of the place. Here I am sitting in my chair, at the small round table we had bought in Britain; here I am admiring this concealed area which I designed, built, decorated and restored to a glory it probably never saw before. A scrap of Earth bearing a thin layer of soil on top. Who knows, if I were to dig deep down into the centre of this plot, where would I end up, down under, maybe? Who knows whether in the fathoms of this soil folds there is a buried treasure, a message in a bottle; a box containing love letters, a wheel, or a coffin with a skeleton inside? Few curious facts I uncovered when shoveling the debris in the act of demolishing the pile of rubbish in the south-eastern corner of the plot, were a pair of torn tights and a condom, I can understand ripping the tights while working in the garden and then deciding to take them off and throw them away there and then, but the condom!?! Well, the latter conjures up a vision of two lovers meeting up in secret for a romantic encounter within the convolutions of a warm summer night. Any other plausible hypotheses, anyone? Aside from the above, the corner by the entrance bore the ancient, rusty lock of a previous gate whose hinges still stick out on the opposite side of the wall. A knife, a spoon, some wrought iron, heavy hooks all caked in a thick layer of oxidized rot. Nothing goes to waste in my garden and all finds are being kept in a glass jar (except for the condom and the torn tights, I swear!) and the discarded gate parts along with kitchen tools, have been inserted into the cracks in between the syenite blocks of the northern wall, where climbers can find a means of winding themselves around or where solar light bulbs can be hung to provide some illumination during our night visits. I am so curious to see my visitors' reaction, when after taking in the garden as a whole, will make time to thoroughly investigate the entire area, inch by inch. I have a feeling they will; they will seek out the details because if my instinct does not fail me (it hardly does) my guests are some kind of rare, special people and there must be a transcendental reason for our prophetic encounter one year ago. I shall find out, I am sure. There are many appealing features, some half hidden, others the focal points, many just a temporary presence such as the ghost-like Passion flower blooms which open up suddenly, last a few hours and vanish with the same speed and element of surprise they had opened up. Every day a colourful bud winks and stares at me from the hidden corners of the garden while the day before, I swear, it was nowhere to be found. This is the difference between a project of an inanimate nature and one with living beings; the latter has the powers of transformation, often sudden, especially following a long spell of rain after a period of hot and prolonged sunshine. The changes are tangible and quite astonishing. A border can be planted with two or three bushes interspersed with perennial herbs and succulents giving the impression of being somewhat empty and, therefore, spurring your eagerness to look for more plants. But make no mistake, because over a mere couple of months the space in between each greenery will have been filled to its capacity and beyond with foliage, stems, new branches, touching, intermingling, entwining and spreading across sideways, upwards, thick and tall, creating the impression of an encroaching forest, difficult to distinguish and to handle. One suddenly feels overwhelmed with the inextinguishable vigour of life, which starts off timidly, a few leaves maybe limp, yellowing, a quivering bloom that spends itself even before seeing the light of day, and so it goes on for days, sometimes weeks on end till, "Boom!" it all explodes in all directions with a richness of colours, scents, textures, shapes, tastes and sensations that all five senses manage to conjure up before such a miracle of Nature. The name labels become buried under the weeping fronds where before they looked like a pet's graveyard, standing up even taller than the plant they describe. I remember my friend helped me to drive the heavy and bulky sunshade, (under which I am sitting right now), up to the entrance to the alleyway and later he was offered a tour of the garden, quite immature, back then. He seemed to appreciate the myriad of labels I had affixed into the ground and commented on their dual English-Latin name. Of course, however clever one can be, all these names can easily escape our brain box. Besides, the herbaceous perennials, disappear in autumn and will not make a come back till the following spring, leaving behind their rhizomes, corms, bulbs, interred in the folds of the earth. How am I to remember where I planted each of them, if not duly marked out with a label? I may dig out in the very spot where they lie, for whatever reason. What a shame to either disturb or to damage a dormant flowery perennial, I say! Well, my friend was delighted with all my efforts, the size and position of my little plot. I wonder what he would make of it now. As soon as the summer holidays are over, I shall invite him again. Isn't it wonderful, exuberant, exceedingly gratifying, where before lay a bare patch of earth, now a profusion of tints, shades, a pool of interweaving and interlacing expressive genes sport themselves and give themselves the element of life? And what about the humble grass? An emerald expanse of waves, emerging jade hues under the blades of a mower. The stalks *bend to the will of the cutting machine to emerge upright again shorter, healthier, a velvety, springy sensation of barefoot steps. So unloved, burnt, poisoned, removed by plucking, stoned over, chocked to death, only to be revered and fed and watered, stroked gently inside some idolized precincts named gardens (but merely as a carpet of turf, still chased off to death if found in a flowering border or inside a herb plot) as opposed to fields or meadows or road verges, not to mention vegetable patches where the wretched blades are vilified, cursed and tormented, made into hay, and fed to animals. Can you imagine a world without grass? A desertified world where only brown soil, white sand or black tarmac and grey cement reign supreme? I love grass and in my garden the native patches have been enriched with luxury seeds to form a soft carpet of a miscellaneous, distinct character such as trefoil, mosses, common grass and wild flowers of Pimpernel, Daisy and Myosotis (forget-me-not).*

A brown little sparrow is clawing itself at the fence when, after eyeing me up and down, attempts little flights like a fledgeling that has just left its nest. There it goes on to the rim of the sprinkling fountain! It hops along it, never taking its black, beady eyes off me, then it cranes its neck into the basin, reaching for the water. A few bounces on the right and it is now enjoying a fresh shower from the water that inclines onto one side. Its beak open, its neck bent backwards as if to utter a few preliminary notes prior to a musical performance but all it manages is a cheerful *"Chirp!"* noise, just a single one, typical of a sparrow, I think. Now declined in numbers, sparrows are a rare sight and this jolly visit is an encouraging sign that although an endangered species, few are still about, leaping and skipping in their variegated brown and white feathery suits like muffins covered in white and dark chocolate chips. I hear footsteps along the public alleyway; there is always someone passing by and I know he or she is not accompanied by a canine friend, because of Rosco's reaction, he merely half opens one of his eyes in sign of acknowledgement, but no further action is required to guard his territory. Of course, steps, they occur behind the northern wall of the garden, and just there, standing on a dark, syenite, cubic block which serves the purpose of a substantial pedestal, there is a foot! Yes, what I thought was a charred human foot, by the shores of the river Elvo, on the plain towards the outskirts of the town. I remember walking back in the direction of my car, after collecting several rocks of interest for their mineral contents, shape and colour, when, out of the corner of my eye I detected an object amongst the ashes of a dead camp fire. In refining my eyesight I had no doubt that what I was looking at, were the charred remains of a human foot. The macabre discovery made me wince there and then, but the dappling effect from the waving canopies above, somewhat deceived my view. I neared the scene and, I screamed with excitement when I realized that the burnt dew-beater was in fact a foot-shaped, syenite stone size 35. It looked very much like a metal last save for the fact it had very little in the way of an ankle like all lasts sport. The first wish was to sandal the foot with an ancient Roman-style footware, but after a fruitless search, one day I came up with a more effective idea of slipping on a size 35 sock! In fact one of my unmatched white socks turned up to be the answer. As I look at the foot now it really gives the impression of being a real one, one lost maybe at the teeth of our nano Pinscher! Rosco raises his eyes as if telepathically aware I am thinking about him, buries his snout in his blanket, and ejects a long sigh as if he were getting tired of such silliness. The same day I found the foot, I also came by a large heart-shaped stone as big as a man's hand, followed a few weeks later by a smaller one. The latter, curiously enough, shed a ventral slice of smaller dimensions than the parent stone, a few millimetres thick, to reveal a hollow heart shape as if it had been carved on purpose. Now both hearts of stone sit back on a syenite cube at the foot of the dry-stone wall pillar half way along the length of the northern wall. I am still intrigued by the feeling that springs from deep inside me every time I shut the gate closed behind me, soon after entering the garden. The act of closing this gate reflects a similar sensation I experienced when, after a shift at the hospital I used to slam the front door of my house shut, thus symbolically shutting out the external world, as a necessary daily ritual in order to gather my strength and find my inner peace. Back then I was confined between the walls of my house and always longed for trees, fountains, meadows, flowers and fresh air. Now, this sacred gate marks the passage from the outside world into an open air, walled room made of the secret life of Nature, stealthily pulsating in this wonderful realm, protected but open to the saturated blue vault above, framed by the green lace of trees and dotted by the sparkling jewels in the bosom of the night. I feel that the ancient dry-stone walls of this inner sanctuary keep out unwanted evil forces. As soon as I step into my garden, very often I remove my shoes and bare foot, on my tip toes I slowly stroll along the grass, discovering a crawling snail (Helix pomatia), its fat, convolute shell gently moving and rotating sideways in unison with the undulating direction of the greyish, slimy foot beneath. The giant Libellula depressa, sporting a brilliant head and flattened, primrose blue abdomen (the male of the species) like a speck of the light cobalt summer sky, fallen onto earth after a storm, hovers from plant to plant to land on top of a bamboo cane. Its huge, compound *eyes gaining a constant three hundred and sixty degrees view of its surroundings; its wings the finest, elaborately worked lace, tiny almost microscopic windows onto the grass below. Some beetles scuttling away, others peacefully mating, their passion gently swayed by the quivering of their leafy abode; the pink, moist end of a wriggling earthworm on the surface of the disturbed soil under the sage. Everyone is welcomed here; I treat the ground with great respect lest I hurt some of its inhabitants. Everyone is safe within these walls and they are free to carry on with their existence, undisturbed as far as possible, by human intervention. Within this harmonious environment I instantaneously calm down, relax, let go of my worries and feel a rush of joy rising from my chest. All I can see here is mine and mine alone and yet the concept of ownership comes with the huge responsibility to care for this concealed place as if I owned someone something. As if I were in debt to someone and only by obeying the sacrosanct laws of Nature, can I fulfill a hidden promise; such is this unrevealed promise that I have been under a spell to create a beautiful, native garden, true to Nature, pacing myself and keeping a log book, a gardening journal where I note all of my achievements and the pending jobs. I act immediately on any idea that formulates itself into my mind, come rain or shine, I have been working in my garden. As I look* around I see a well-designed, well-accomplished green space which has by far exceeded my wildest expectations. I just wonder whose voice I keep hearing inside my head, that very same voice that beckoned me into this garden, the first time I had a glimpse through the gate and the crack in the wall. What a day it was, one of the best in my life. Why of all places this one; and the miraculously swift deal with the previous owner. So unlikely to happen in normal circumstances given the fact that this garden came with the house it always belonged to. These thoughts keep surfacing and gnawing at my intellect and they even go deeper into my subconscious mind where I hope I'll find an answer soon.

The clock chimes again the tenth hour, its sound echoing wide and wider, it lingers with its deep resonant tones to dissolve as quickly as it came to be airborne.

My guests will be here soon, now. I could be at the Chelsey Flower Show, or to be about to open the doors of my gated property to the National Trust, for the first time, offering my treasures to the scrutiny of the judges. There is nothing missing, nothing else I could think of. Yes, the National Trust, our beloved great British institution. That's the one thing I have been missing since leaving Britain in May 2019. By then we had paid our full yearly fee so we still qualified for our membership cards renewals and the properties handbook. The latter was sent to our Italian address accompanied by a thank you letter for our faithful membership over many years. I felt like crying, deprived of what had been my lifeline during my time off work. Walking into any National Trust property had always felt like visiting trusted friends, their knowledge, professional entrepreneurial abilities and their warm, welcoming smiles, now a thing of the past. Countless hours spent around those amazing properties, through the changing seasons. The mansions with the fantastic stately rooms containing all the appointments pertaining to their epoch they belonged to; the kitchen, the bedrooms, drawing, music, tea rooms, extensive libraries of ancient, polished, wooden cases; the smell and patina of a bygone era all brought back to life with unequalled mastery by the management and their entourage of erudite and passionate volunteers. Then the gardens, parks, orchards, vegetable patches; meadows and shallow chalk streams, pools and ponds, rich woodlands and fountains of all shapes, character and water capacity, everything lovingly tended by zealous gardeners and retired such more volunteers all toiling in a concerted manner to recreate and maintain the glorious green retreats of the past. And what about the shop with all kinds of memorabilia, sweets, local produce, books, brochures, post cards, clothing, toys, toiletries and plants displayed in the outdoors courtyard. The coffee shop, a mouth watering flaunt of sweet and savoury snacks and meals made with local produce from their gardens cooked from scratch by proficient, inventive cooks who source ancient cookery texts and tap into their own imagination to concoct the exquisite dishes to be found nowhere else. And last but not least, in fact foremost as far as I am concerned, the jewel in the crown, the second-hand book shops thanks to the generous donations of local people and, with increased frequency now, from closing-down public libraries (Alas!). The National Trust motto: 'Give an old book a new home', has penetrated my heart like an arrow and because of my love of books of miscellaneous interest, history, archeology, English literature, art, painting, bric-a-brac collecting, I was always attracted to those book shops like a magnet. Treasure troves of antique and specialized texts, offered for a mere twenty pence or free, arranged on a stall outside the shop entrance, a notice stating 'Books for pulping, please help yourself'. I always wondered on what criterion a book was for pulping when the ones being sold inside the shop were of equal quality, same era and often same subject. And I never asked the reason why. The thrill of sitting down under the sunshade by an ancient wall, bedecked in vibrant creepers, just opposite the coffee shop. A hot, smoking mug of strong, black coffee and a cheese scone by the side and a pile of newly purchased old books to peruse at leisure. People strolling by, smiling, absorbed in their own thoughts, no doubt, or perhaps bemused at watching me buried behind my stack of printed material, hardly noticing their presence, engrossed in my own world of literature. I have experienced no joy of similar intensity anywhere in Italy with the exception of my English-style garden. Yes, the one I am sitting in right now. Its walls and the arrangements of assorted accoutrements that blend well with one another and their environment, in my mind are reminiscent of the vegetable garden in His Majesty King Charles's Highgrove Estate. For that very reason, I have called my little hideaway Little HighGrove. Just like over there, the Genius Loci, otherwise known as the Green Man, is an essential feature to promote constant rebirth and regeneration of all living beings within the walls. I have painted an oak leaves disgorging man with the sun and the spring fountain in A3 size as the vital elements of life. Another collage of a Green Man, I made of brilliant autumn maple leaves, again in A3 size. Both creations will eventually find a place on the walls of a future addition to my garden, my spiritual retreat, in the form of a garden shed. Of course, when a garden is not attached to your house, you cannot enjoy it throughout the year in all weathers. I have a fascination with wooden huts fronted by french windows covered with double-glazed panes, and lots of firms make pre-fabricated ones but I shall have to wait till the autumn. A three by two and a half metres cabin will suit me right, sited a few inches along the eastern wall where the neighbour's mortar chicken coup stands. It will be one and a half metres away from the opening of the entry gate, hence giving way to a narrowed passage between the northern wall of the shed to be and the edge of the southern-facing border. At that point, I want to place a gated wrought iron arch, later covered in climbers of my choice, to give access to the garden proper. This feature is going to be a real triumph which I cannot yet share with my guests today. They will be met with a new, exciting surprise in due course. Yes, I call it a garden shed, but in fact I think of it and will use it as my country bolt-hole, because aside from housing a few tools such as two rakes, two spades, the manual lawn mower (Philip Larkin the great lyricist of lawn mowing would be proud of me) to avoid damaging both the grass and the creatures who dwell amongst its blades and creases; one fork, one garden trowel, a short-handled hand rake and a couple of brushes (aside for a short-handled and long-handled shears), a hand brush and a large, soft hair brush to clean the path and border stones. I shall be dwelling inside it with a chair, a small table and a means to store some painting, writing, and reading material. Maybe a couple of shelves will accommodate some essential gardening books, coffee is to be added to the happiness equation and a good brew needs energy which, in this modern times, can be harnessed directly from the sun by means of a solar panel placed on the south-facing side of the summer house roof. I can already see myself spending the whole day and even night, weather allowing, in my enchanted place; watching the rain fall onto my beloved plants, the features I added, being varnished clear and the pots and vases collecting water as the dripping goes on. The freshness of the air will hit my senses when I open the french windows onto a drenched world at the end of a summer storm; the blue sky upside down into the rain drops that cling to the leaves; barefoot I shall venture out onto a soaking loan weary less I tread on the creatures who are enjoying the same luxury: snails, slugs, earthworms, all sharing a congenial flake of the terrestrial crust within its safe, wall-guarded precincts. Have I ever felt more free, more accomplished, more humbled and grateful than this garden ever afforded me to feel? I doubt it. Cicero understood the intrinsic nature of a happy, erudite soul, combining books with gardens. In fact his quote stating "If you have a garden and a library, you have everything you need", goes further than conceiving two separate spaces. Cicero, like all ancient Roman scholars, used to teach in his beautiful gardens and to walk around their green, enclosed spaces with a book in his hands, reading, pondering, meditating and producing new philosophical thoughts, besides teaching his students in the shade of majestic olive trees. Well, that is how I feel, when steeped into the soul of my garden, the bustling world outside and solitude and contentment inside me. Books, my early life's love which has been growing as the years go by, the emotion of opening an old book, like a first encounter; the excitement of discovering what lies hidden between its yellowed, stained or mottled pages, the smell of foregone decades, left lying somewhere, forgotten, cherished or unwanted, just perused or fully absorbed, intact or bearing the penciled notes of a keen reader; the soft touch of time lifting in a quickly disposed cloud of veneer when a curious mind decides to disturb its secrets, to open its treasures and page after page the ancient scent is released in rich wafts to remind us that books, feel, smell, tell, show and reveal a hidden world, just a tiny fraction of someone's views, experience, emotions to be shared with equal enthusiasm, sadness, eagerness. These tiny portions of universal consciousness buried within the pages of our friends, the old books, to open a window into the past, our past, of earlier eras that shaped the lives we live today. Books, beloved books, voices, sighs, sorrows, laughter and more. I hold a huge library at home, the majority of the books, precious second-hand ones mostly came to me as cheap bargains from various National Trust properties; some of these treasured wells of knowledge will make their home into my summer house inside my garden. Like Cicero, I have the best of both worlds and I can call myself both fortunate and privileged. Through the dappled stirrings of the Passion flower leaves, almost close to the ground, I spot one open bloom, a rare botanical beauty, splaying its green sepals to reveal a deep blue crown inside, surmounted by a precious stone studded with yellow and purple gems, amazingly complex a structure of ephemeral existence as each flower last but one day. This climber has been shooting off in all directions, fanning out along the supporting net and tenaciously clinging to it with its close-winding leafy tendrils. Dotted along the shoots are tens of green, closed blooms, but for some reason only two or maximum three flowers open up at one time along the creeping stems. Meanwhile, the three-poled support around the amphora, is slowly being dressed with green, lacy hosiery, crawling up the three legs eager to reach the top from where a silver lantern dangles. Too early for the blooms on these jolly, recently rooted Clematis and Honeysuckle plants, but their dark and light green interlocking sprays are enough to bring life to stainless steel supports, like delightful pole dancers embracing the posts onto which they firmly grip and climb.

Something is moving near the Daphne odora, a brown animal is arching its back which is sticking up more and more as I look. A rat? I cannot think of anything else. I must move closer to scare it off, although presently I am more fearful than whatever is bloating itself up at the foot of my Jasmine sempervirens. As I cautiously walk towards it, on high alert, I notice three more of these creatures scattered along my border; 'Good Heavens!' I never thought such a scourge could blight my garden. Surely, up to now we have lived in peace; surely theses animals were there before, although undisclosed within the creases of the earth. I freeze dead in front of the offenders, horrified at the havoc they have wreaked with my succulents. Some lie on their side, their roots in the air; others are covered in soil, their rosettes marred till the next downpour washes it all away, to reveal their plump, green petals rimmed with red tints again. A mole or perhaps more than one have produced four mounds of freshly dug earth with total disregard for my poor plants. Not only did they not care but they have acted now, yes, because two hours ago the ground was flat; of all times now that I am waiting to greet my guests. My disappointment is soon replaced by acceptance and a delighted spirit of enquiry for this rather fetching, little, blind mammal, the Mole, who utilizes his scoop-like forefeet armed with powerful claws for digging tunnels. Their pink, elongated snouts poking out of their shallow burrows, when they surface from their deeper tunnels. Well, never mind. Moles mostly feed on invertebrates and there is a rich variety of prey here at the restaurant, to choose from. It is not a choice of restaurants but a natural food chain. Besides, moles turn the soil thus allowing both air and rain to penetrate deep, which can only be beneficial for my plants' roots network system. So, equipped with a trowel, I demolish each mole hill, redistributing the soil and covering the affected areas with bark chips. I have no doubt this square of Earth is Nature's haven. I have always nurtured a fascination for creatures who disdain the direct light of the sun and lead their existence in heavenly solitude several inches inside the depth of the underground world. Their homes, a complex network of tunnels or a simple straight burrow away from the preying eyes and intentions of potential predators. One thus orthopteron, the black Field cricket (Gryllus campestris), that even though sharing meadows and fields with hundreds of other fellow melody producers, it keeps itself to itself displaying a territorially defensive character, to take care of its slanting burrow, some four inches long. I have been studying and observing these orthoptera since I was a child and have been keeping them inside terraria where the environment and micro climatic conditions are very similar to their natural world. However, this time, with the garden available, I thought I might seed crickets as one might seed flowers. With that in mind, I caught several males and a few females, the males for their sonorous chirping sound and the females for reproduction. Gryllus campestris's life only spans twelve months, they are born miniature adults out of eggs and undergo several moultings as nymphs till they reach their fifth nymphal instar and this period is spent inside their burrows, overwintering, to re-emerge in early spring and moult into sexually mature adults equipped with chirping elytra (the male) and a long ovipositor (the female). They have round shiny heads, with two glossy, black beads for eyes. They are beautiful creatures, protagonists of several children's stories for their wisdom and appealing demeanour. I could now reproduce them in my lawn and spend the summer evenings listening to their modulating love calls. I, therefore, brought all my catches to my garden and inserted them into single burrows I made by means of a round brush handle, more or less the diametre of a slanting cricket's burrow. I was delighted to watch my crickets, all adults, sleep at the entrance to their hole, antennae prostrated in the sunshine. Then, as they felt my footfall vibrate on the ground, they bolted back into their burrow. But my joy was short-lived because after two weeks, one by one, they all disappeared; with time their holes filled up with fresh earth. A failed experiment worth investigating further in the future. A puff of breeze has carried a whiff of grass and leaves over to my nostrils. As I look in the western direction of my garden, trying to track down its origin, I am almost sure it comes from the heavy pruning we did two days ago. Indeed, over the green netting, metallic fence of the western aspect, is a wild, overgrown, intermingling forest of giant brambles, small false Acacia trees, fast growing maple and ash seedlings, all competing for light and in so doing forcing their way either over my fence or through the holes of the net. Time to act because the neighbours would not budge! Better to keep on good friendly terms with potentially awkward neighbours than having arguments for the sake of upholding my neighbouring rights. Using a four metres long, telescopic pole with a rake attachment, my husband grabbed the offensive vegetation and pulled it forward, while, with a pair of sharp, long-handled secateurs, I chopped off as much as I could reach. The result is excellent and it will keep all the invasive greenery at bay, for a while, at least. Only two months ago a gardener armed with a notoriously noisy, petrol-driven strimmer, appeared from behind our fence. He greeted us politely and told us he had been hired to clear the briars. However, he would leave the ones near the neighbours' entry gate to the passage, till next time. His aggressive pruning left us vulnerable to preying eyes through our metallic fence, and the episode acted as a catalyst for our next action plan which consisted in buying some PVC fake foliage rolls, two metres tall to affix to our fencing thus restoring the privacy we were enjoying before. While tending to the job, we cast an eye over the neighbours' property and discovered an amazing passage. A narrow, low corridor between our fence which sits on a lower dry-stone wall and the metallic rusty fence on the other side. The passage has two accesses, one entry point from the alleyway via a narrow, tall, rot-covered, iron gate and at the end of the passage, an old weather-beaten, wooden door which gives access to the neighbours' garden over our southern dry-stone wall delimiting the border between mine and my neighbours' properties. Over the door is and arch of ancient bricks, covered on top with syenite blocks onto which old style roof tiles are arranged. The whole composition is surmounted with large-leaved, creepy Ivy, whose long sprays swing intermittently in the breeze. Above, the weeping, gnarled branches of the pear and plum trees cast long shadows along the passage and afforded an eerie obscurity which conjured up an atmosphere of tantalizing secrecy. Immediately, my mind traveled to the 'Secret Garden' by Frances Hodgson Burnett and a shiver of thrilling emotion ran down my spine. How beautiful, how exciting to be witnessing the perfect, mysterious passage with a concealed garden door one foot away from my property. It was lying undiscovered and maybe hopefully one day someone will clear the infestation that is keeping it a prisoner of Nature. But the door was not closed, it had been left ajar by the gardener, no secret key was to be found inside some wet crevice of the stone wall. The door was open, and through its chink of light I could see the garden beyond; a green lawn with mature pear trees, bound on the western aspect by a dry-stone wall. The fascination with this secret garden has, nevertheless, stuck with me and, after reading 'The Secret Garden' only last year, I feel so happy, so privileged to have been privy to this lovely garden feature, a sloping, concealed passage leading up to an Ivy-covered, wooden door in the wall. I remember one of my acquaintances telling me that in this village, which consists of a central thoroughfare giving rise to ancient medieval buildings on both its sides, there lie hundreds of hidden plots through archways, gates and doors and passersby would never imagine such beauty exists. Now I know what he meant. I remember the first glimpse I got of my garden, initially through a crack in the wall and then a narrow gate that suddenly appeared like a window in a wall. Only now I know what it means to be part of this hidden world with the sky as the roof and green plants as the walls while the floor of velvety sensations of live chlorophyll under my bare feet. I have already witnessed the four seasons since acquiring my garden in October 2022 but truth to be told, this little square plot started to take shape as a proper garden in February 2023 and the seasons to come will roll in and go leaving their mark like a paint brush on a canvas.

Like the shards of a broken mirror, the sun shimmers through the dense foliage of the Acacia wood, the pinnate leaves tremble and throb in a green marine-like wave, gently whipped by the breeze; thankfully the canopies above afford some much needed shade in the summer; then comes winter, the bare skeletal branches will allow the low, weaker sunshine to reach the lawn, while the stone-walls absorb the energy to be radiated back into the atmosphere during the night, thus benefitting my climbers and border perennials. What a lovely invention dry-stone walls are. Mine are primarily made of syenite blocks, white and grey speckled blocks, their power of energy absorption from the sun is intense and the amount they radiate back in the night is almost equal to their rate of intake during daytime. It follows that their surface is so hot as to fool plants into thinking it is a rather dark but sunny night and their proliferation is promoted faster than expected. Also, the direction of the wind is mostly from east to west, so once the wind has tumbled down from the top of the eastern wall it can easily escape through the western fence where only the

Pyracantha hedge will act as a breathable barrier. In other words, my garden is situated within precincts that offer the ideal growing conditions all year round.

'Who is blowing a raspberry? And then another, making one spin around towards the gate? Could they be my guests?' The dog lifts his head and pricks his ears; looks up into the swinging foliage and, with a sigh, goes back to sleep, but only temporarily. He wakes up and I follow his gaze, sure enough, another raspberry is ejected from the thick of the green. A magpie arguing with a counterpart responding in kind from the bough of a nearby tree. The quarrel goes on for a few minutes getting louder and louder, and then a flash of black and white plumage darts into the sky, the two contenders chasing each other further afield. But something curiously pea-like has just landed on the extended branches of the Bay Laurel tree. Baffled, I rise from my chair, cautiously I approach the scene. Oh, what a beauty! A short, light-brown jacket, like a little parachute, an emerald green vest over a peridot yellowish-green leotard from which well-toned, slim limbs of rich auburn tints stick out. The face of light complexion as kiwi jelly, supporting two little bulges with a black dot in the middle which move in unison with the rotation of its head. The tiny acrobat hangs by a thread of its foot on the margin of a leaf with the remaining feet in the act of preening itself. And it hangs there, gently buffeted by the odd puff of breeze. This high wire walker is not scared of heights and comfortably carries out its self-caring routine without a single worry in the world. A green Bush cricket! Quite a rarity these days. It's amazing how that little rucksack-like feature on its dorsum, its elytra, can produce such a loud tune of chief maracas player. Two little yellow extrusions show on each side of the elytra, no doubt part of its complex stridulating apparatus, looking more like some extra clothing to wear stuffed into its knapsack in a hurry, should the weather close in. I just marvel at this little wonder from Nature, so beautiful, so elegantly camouflaged, against the rich summer greenery. These are the joys of owning an organic garden, where creatures can be observed in their native habitat undisturbed. Such ephemeral lives, and yet Nature goes to such an extent to produce striking jewels with intricate details of differing shades of colour, all to contribute to the diversity of both plant and animal life. Even the dullest of organism, if observed with the due attention of a Nature lover, reveals extraordinary hidden characteristics that merge into a whole and often blend with its environment. Take the red slug (Arion rufus) I can see creeping under my sage bush; a slimy, red foot a couple of inches long and yet, in the absence of a hard shell, it enjoys a soft mantle instead, where its visceral contents are enclosed in its dorsum. There, a large pneumostoma or respiratory *pore, opens and closes at intervals in the act of breathing. Its body is a furrowed, muscular foot with a distinguished rim that pumps in an undulating locomotion, secreting mucus as it moves forward. Its tentacles surmounted by two black pinhead eyes. It is classed as one of the worst pests by horticulturalists but in fact it can thrive in my garden because there is nothing that tantalizes its radula. The other day, when I lifted one of the terracotta sherds which lean against the dry-stone wall, I found a nest of Leopard slugs' (Limax maximus) white opalescent eggs, a grey type of large slug with black stripes and dots all over its body. What an exciting discovery, yes, because the rain always brings out the red slugs and the rich variety of snails. Incidentally, one small snail is crawling up the pot which contains some herbaceous plants I collected last March and planted as an experiment. They all thrived and one I enjoyed watching as time went by, was the Lunaria annua with its vividly purple inflorescences that now have turned into ripe pods, oval, white-silvery, flat, paper-like structures, formed of three layers where the brown seeds are found. They look like tiny opaque mirrors mounted on a woody, flimsy frame. Their proper name is Siliques and the sound of the word 'Siliques', evokes a sensation of silky medallions quivering in the breeze. Earlier on the Siliques changed from green to yellow, crimson and orange, all nuances of the four colours* in between, blended in each and every pod which, when pierced by the sun looked beautifully translucent and dotted with four or five, dark seeds inside. I shall try to grow more of these annual plants from the seeds I am gradually collecting.

It is July, a quintessential month of rich flowery borders, bushes and trees. However, as the year progresses, the first signs of the 'Season of mists and mellow fruitfulness' as sang by John Keats in his renowned poem, is already poignantly here, in the large pears dangling from the neighbouring, overhanging trees boughs; the small, local plums of a brilliant bluish-purple colour again hanging about the eastern wall, that have started falling with a 'thump-thump' noise at intervals. The Lunaria seeds are ready to be released into the air, yes, the very air I am breathing is not so effervescent, full of expectations and exciting hesitancy for what new life may bring; now that lively feeling is being gradually replaced by a kind of broody melancholy that settles around the garden where no big surprises are in store but where time is hanging still, having raised into blooming, sprouting, climbing, crawling, rooting, growing to reach a climax of voluptuous beauty which will slowly fade as autumn knocks on the iron bars of my garden's gate. At this time of the year, the strong scent from the nearby wood undergrowth is prominent, it penetrates the wind that comes and goes now gentle, then more impetuous as a premonition of harsh days to come. The mountain top is mostly shrouded in a thick cape of grey moisture that only lifts in the middle of the day, to fall back gravely mid-afternoon. The pods of the Black Locust Acacia (Robinia) trees have also started to fall gently onto the lawn, their hard-cased seed structures, a useful addition to my borders bark chips layer, after raking the turf. Who said a 'gardener's work is never done?' Well, spot on! There is not a single day I come to the garden that I either weed, rake or provide support for some leaning stems, or clean, mow the lawn, trim its edges, brush the stones and so on and so forth. But, I would not have it any other way. I love my new life inside my roofless, green room; it feels healthy, free, creative, natural, live and very relaxing. Gardening, painting and writing is now my way of life. My plants are my new patients and the invertebrates they support, are their close relations, all to be looked after and when need be, to nurse back to their ideal health. A far cry from the four walls of the anaesthetic room and operating theatre where I was confined almost all day long, throughout the year. How many times my mind wandered through green meadows along the shores of mountain streams and trickling brooks; on top of a peak, to a woodland when, a whiff of mowed grass came through the vents of the hospital air conditioning? That scent was irresistible and I dreamt and hoped with all my heart that one day I might enjoy as much fresh air within the open confines of a walled garden as I had endured the foul air, heavy with anaesthetic gases and diathermy smoke within the close environment of my clinical area. That day is now! I have made it. I am lucky, and grateful for the new lease of life I am now relishing. That is the reason why the guests I am eagerly waiting for, to welcome warmly into my garden this morning, mean so much to me. For all the promises in the world, this dream-come-true is second to none. I remember that day we came along searching for the owners of what is now my beloved garden. That day is etched into my mind, like an ancient script on an ostracon; it is my keepsake lying inside my soul, being nourished as time goes by so as to be revisited at will like a painting in a permanent gallery, its beauty growing with each visit and so the fondness and yearning when away from it. The exhortation by the matron in the household in the house above the alleyway: "Giorgio go down to see, there are some people interested in our garden." I heard her voice and raised my eyes to a small, open window at the top floor of the house opposite the gate at which we had stopped to make enquiries. A smiling lady, leaning on the window sill, seemed to know what we were talking about and she was keen to help. Too keen, in fact. But why? I was flabbergasted. Seconds later, her son in law strode towards us with a key in his hand and he was joined by his son soon afterwards. The two gentlemen unlocked the rusty gate which needed a good push to open and let us into this amazing seventy five square metres, a green plot surrounded on three sides by dry-stone walls, with a green metallic fence tensed between two red-bricked pillars on the fourth one. Paradise! And they started telling me that the grass grew very quickly; and the briars pierced the western wall perimeter and needed pulling out regularly. Moles also appeared quite frequently.

"Do you want to use it as a vegetables garden?"

"No, absolutely not! I want to design and plant an English garden".

"Oh, wow, how interesting. However, there is no irrigation system here, only water-collecting tubs and the nearby fountain".

"That would suit me just fine", I replied full of hope.

"OK, then let's go and talk to the owner."

'The owner? I wondered.

We were ushered into a three-storey house, inside a courtyard by the entrance to the alleyway and, on the second floor kitchen I met the lady at the window. Her name, Maria, was really taken by my garden project and listened carefully to what I intended to do with the plot.

'How much would I want to spend?' I did not know, I preferred leaving the decision to them. I recognized true friendship, honesty and amiability through this lady's eyes and the welcoming attitude of her family; I could not be mistaken. She said she would meet me half way with the price and I was quick to add that even if no agreement was reached, I would still be keen in getting to know them and becoming their friend.

"Friendship is the most beautiful gift of all", Maria said. And I believed her. Maria added she would contact her daughter in Milan immediately so that the sale operation through the surveyor could be started. As I walked out of that house I knew I was going to be the proud owner of that square of paradise. I felt it in my bones. And indeed, two months later, at the notary's office, Maria's daughter, who was given power of attorney, and I signed the legal papers which led to the land registry documents bearing my rightful name on the plot. It should have been Maria, the legitimate proprietor of the garden to sign the papers off. I learnt that day a fracture of her femur confined her to hospital which meant having a notary in Milan to draw up a Power of Attorney document and physically visit Maria in hospital for her legal signature. It is obvious that the plot was basically given to me with no real profit on their behalf whatsoever, besides they were happy to proceed on the fixed date when, as I remember suggesting we could have waited for Maria to be discharged from the hospital and sell the property at a later date. Where do you find people of such personal integrity these days? To say it is a rarity, is an understatement. But the question kept recurring, "Why?" Why does a family with a house that comes with a piece of land want to get rid of the latter? And why was not the plot put up for sale in the first instance since it sounded much like they were waiting for a buyer but no sale notice was hanging from the gate? The mystery was unravelled by my guest. That mystery translated itself into a bond of love for what has turned into a shared dream. This has been a most bizarre story of a garden and its owners who, for twenty seven years waited to bestow a gift of rebirth and tender loving care to what they consider a true extension of their family's affections. But was it really so? I had been longing to own a garden in Italy within walking distance of my house all my life. The two gardens that came with our English properties, a springboard of exercise and practice into what is now my unquestionable masterpiece. Actually, the one aspect of my garden I really enjoy is the rustic look of the stones I used to delimit my borders from the lawn edge. Aside from my family of tortoises, well established by the mid north-facing wall footfall, the bumpy, large stones can always act as a tortoise body to which an expressive stone head can be leant against. Such is the case for three of the stones along the south-facing border, a touch of ongoing creativity. The sun is now high up in the sky and the shadow cast by the sunshade is getting smaller. What was a pale wash of sunshine at 08:00 o'clock this morning, is gradually turning into a glowing, hot furnace and I can feel the heat beating down my neck. Hopefully, by the time my guests arrive, there will be enough shade around the table so that we can all take shelter for a chat and exchange impressions. Luckily, good, old Saint Fiacre is protected from the sunlight by the long, arching fronds of the Dryopteris; and incidentally, before too long, exactly on September the 1st is Saint Fiacre's Day. I must celebrate with a bounty of flowers and herbs present in my garden. Perhaps I could make a garland to hang around his neck to match the one he permanently wears around his wrist. Good, old Saint Fiacre. Faith is a powerful sentiment, strong enough to change your life for the better. I say this because the only reason why I bought a statue of the saint is to ensure he blesses me with the ability to care for my garden and to ensure nothing untowards happens to it. In fact, only last week, a hurricane-force storm with gales, lashing rain and hail beat down on the garden. The morning after I came in to assess the situation, I do not know why, confident everything was perfectly OK and, as soon as I opened the gate 'Alas!', my fright or flight hormone sent my heart racing at the horrifying scene before my eyes. I could not believe I was let down by the Spirit of the Place. Then I came to my senses and started reasoning logically, because, unfortunately murphy's law had struck or at that very moment I was inclined to rely on sods law, such was the state of mind I was in. I looked around the garden's walls and further beyond. No, nowhere else had bad luck landed, just here! My neighbour's plum tree had keeled over the south-western corner of my garden and everything was buried underneath it. I froze on the spot, a sinking feeling was digging a whole at the bottom of my stomach. I was unable to accept the fact that after all these years, that huge branch of the Prunus tree had waited for me to bedeck the corner before falling on both ornaments and plants. With bated breath, one step at a time as if in slow motion, I moved towards the thick canopy that touched to the ground. As I was approaching the scene, I started to discern the orange terracotta amphora, the green poles around which my Honeysuckle and Clematis had been winding themselves for several weeks now, successfully; my fake pond with its rocky shores and the cherub head with the looking-glass, small window into the valley. They were all there and at first sight looked crushed under the weight of the plum tree. With utmost care, I began to move the branches apart in order to gain a better view of the damage to the structures beneath. My surprise stunned me speechless, only my thoughts went to both my spiritual entities with my deepest sense of gratitude I ever felt for non-conformist deities. Had they both worked a miracle that I was witnessing with my heart drumming in my chest? Had they performed a magical, mystical, supernatural trick to overturn the outcome of sods law? It certainly looked so. I raised my eyes to the tree and realized that it was still standing upright. What had fallen over, however thick and potentially destructive, was one of its main branches which upon snapping off it had taken part of the main bole with it. The rupture looked horrible and I felt for the poor tree. No sign of charring was present which excluded the accidental striking of lightening. It was clear from the gaping wound that the heavy branch got severed under its own weight during the powerful storm. Its characteristics were very significant in the events that followed the moment of its detachment: a forked branch made of two main boughs from which several small branches and twigs radiated in a dense profusion bearing a thick crown of leaves. On observation I then noticed that the poles were sticking out at the top through this section of the canopy and the wider angle of the two converging boughs was containing my garden's structures, as if in a very tight embrace, a frightening clasp around two of the three poles. Therefore, instead of being smashed head-on, my beloved plants along with all the ornaments, got wedged in! A glimmer of hope dawned upon me and, having braced myself for the worst, I was now gaining strength that surged from the desire to lift the suffocating fronds with more optimism. Whew! Boo-yah! I had no better words to express my feelings of relief and astonishment on discovering that all of my garden features, plants and their supporting structures laid buried completely intact! Yes, that fall was totally uneventful aside from some bruising of the Honeysuckle (Lonicera) climbing plant leaves, and a scatter of plums and leaves on the ground. 'Then, this really is a magic garden!', I said aloud; all my creativity and hard work had simply been temporarily concealed under a curtain of fronds without any untoward consequences save for the tree itself, that stood pitifully wounded and, no doubt, in pain. Relieved, but still in shock, I thanked my spiritual guardians and started a network of calls in order to clear the mess as quickly as possible. My neighbour over the eastern wall was extremely helpful and gave me the telephone number of the tree owner, my southern wall neighbour. The latter, whom I had not met to that point came up to assess the situation immediately and, together, we managed to contact a well-known individual (who turned out to be a 'jack of all trades and master of none' type) who was available to come the day after armed with a turn-of-the-last-century, petrol-driven chain saw. My trusted friend, the woodman, had unfortunately for myself, just left for one week's holiday and thus was of no use whatsoever. Meticulously, and as careful as a nurse while trimming the nails of a new-born baby, I grabbed my hand-shears and started pruning the thick intricacy of twigs and smaller branches so as to clear away the screen that covered the evidence. Also I wanted to ensure our handyman could see what he was going to do and that he would realize he had to move with due care and attention in order to avoid damaging my property. Would it not have been preposterous if, after coming out of the storm unscathed, my bedecked corner got damaged during the process of clearing up? Well, it was no laughing matter, and the events that followed my organizing of the day for the tidying up were amply indicative of a potential catastrophe which might have exceeded the storm. Hence my very disturbed night prior to the arrival of the handyman, a most amiable chap with no knowledge of tree pruning, whatsoever, let alone of green plants climbing up a fence pole, used as he was to just strimming away beds and fields, ditches and courtyards in the middle of summer when the grass had reached the height of a five years old. The appointment was one morning two days after the storm at 09:00 am. Of course, he arrived at 09:30. My husband, whom I sent out on a recce, met the guy while walking to the end of the alleyway; he caught him sitting on the fountain rim, his Ape car parked against the wall, swearing his head off as he was changing an obviously incompetent chain saw with a better one and the plastic cover kept falling off. At least he was here, I patted myself. A few minutes later he barged into the garden through the open gate and, without any ceremony, half listening to my pleas to pay attention to the delicate structures lying under the canopy he was about to cut through, he switched on his infernal tool and starting hacking off branch after branch and, as he did so, he pulled and dragged them off the fallen bough. I sat on my garden chair, biting my nails unable to take my eyes off the sawdust and chips of wood flying everywhere, steadily covering the ground under a soft, conspicuous layer, like snow drifting against the wall on a freezing December afternoon. Then as things could not have got any worse, he decided to fetch his step ladder, plonked it behind the amphora, climbed up it with the saw running in one hand, he hoisted himself up onto the unstable tiles on top of the stone-wall, trying to reach the proximal end of the bough at the point where it had broken off. He then brandished his chain saw (which rattled on and off as if it were to stop any minute) and stretched upwards, his power tool jerking erratically, the scene from the horror film, 'Leatherface'. The visceral pitch of the machine penetrated my brain, my chest, every single muscle in my body; every single fibre tensing and snapping with the drilling cacophony of the deafening decibels produced by the motor. I thought he would not dare to tug at the fat bough thus pulling it down and haul it over the wall into my property. But he did! A huge pile of wood and leaves was now lying on the lawn but he did not chuck any of the vegetation over the fence where the brambles are; oh no! He dragged them, two, even three at a time across the lawn and through my narrow gate, beating and ripping my grass in the process and he disposed of the mutilated limbs into the wood nearby. As soon as he came back, I thanked him profusely and told him I could carry on cleaning the rest of the debris myself with no need for further help. Before leaving he commented: "Incredible how that bough wedged itself around your garden stuff without damaging anything in the least. A miracle, really...".

"Yes, that is very true", I replied, with my full faith restored, all doubts brushed away with a sense of guilt. Now, beginning to relax, I started to remove all the debris, the saw dust, the leaves from around my garden items and rewound my slightly bruised Honeysuckle around its support. Half an hour later, the scene that presented itself to my eyes was astonishing, nothing had happened, nothing at all. It was a miracle and I believed in it with all my heart.

Only the south-western corner was brighter than before with fewer branches overhanging the amphora. Now, as peace had fallen again into my garden, and only the songs of the birds and the rushing waters of the stream down below filled the silence, I was aware that this accident had somewhat shaken my perception through the trauma I had endured and slowly, a fear of potential danger lurking above, started creeping inside me, to inflame my recently frayed nerves. I raised my eyes and instead of the ethereal canopies sparkling with diamonds in the sky, I saw a heavy, green, menacing umbrella topping and swaying over the tall boles, now moving this way now that way, towering above me the whole length and breath of the garden. I was now filled with a premonition of impending catastrophic consequences should I let destiny take its course. The very recent and now more frequent storms with gale-force wind and torrential rain and hail, might cause the Robinias above to topple and the trunks inclination is in the direction of my garden. Horrified I stared at those giants, living beings which I no longer admired for their majestic beauty, but feared their powerful and unpredictable behaviour, under their mighty physical presence. Only then I felt the irrepressible urge to act on the prospective danger to life that the trees posed. They belong to the town hall as they grow on the public land; however, knowing how uninterested and apathetic the local authorities are, I decided to take the reins of the situation into my hands. What happened next is quite extraordinary. But, yet again, the good Spirits of my garden came to my aid to preserve the intact identity of the land they inhabit and protect, and the probably offensive trees no longer pose a threat to human, plant or animal life, that is within the mystical boundaries of my beloved garden. I want to believe it. Two days after the eventful clearing of the fallen branch, I could not stop mulling over the threat of those trees and consequently I resorted to harness the help of as many bodies as possible not just with a view to sorting out my problem as soon as possible, but also to formally log my complaint so as to create a robust trail of evidence that I was serious about taking action against the potential harm falling trees can cause. I needed people in authority and with the precise remit in the matter of forestry and land management to risk assess my claims and to record the outcome. Only then I would be covered in the eventuality of those trees accidental fall and there would be no doubt I would be entitled to a due compensation for the damages suffered. However, deep in my heart I hoped it would not have to come to that, I would have rather hoped people would come to their senses, understand the situation and proceed to either prune or to fell the affronting giants. But, whom to go to first? My neighbour had suggested I contact the manager in charge of the land management housed in the town hall technical department. However, the second neighbour sneered at the proposal: "Four years ago I was a friend of the Mayor; I pointed out back then, the state of dereliction in which the footpath and the woodland were lying in, and guess what? He did not pay any heed to my complaint. I wrote a letter and included the pertinent photographic material. To no avail. Nothing. He did not care one iota".

Stress, loneliness, isolation, trees falling, crashing down, storms, lightening, the earth...I love Nature... I cannot wait; birds chirping, Passion flowers opening, dogs barking, everything seemed to be disturbing me, everything and everyone was conspiring against me. My anxiety levels were sky high. There was no support for citizens in this village, region, Country even? If a private owner's vegetation encroaches on public land he/she is made to take action on pain of hefty fines; if the threat, on the other hand, is posed by publicly owned items, they do not comply with the health and safety regulations they have drafted up themselves, they do as they please, when and if it suits them and still walk about the village holding their head up with authority and pride. I spent two days and two nights worrying about what to do next without a clue as how to go about it, whom to turn to. Because of the local authority reputation, I had better turn to my friend the woodman, yes;

he knows how to fell trees, he can help. He did it in the past and I was grateful. He could come surreptitiously in the dead of night and by means of a sharp axe he could adopt an open-notch technique and direct the felling of the tree; two or even three trees would be even better, using the domino effect because they are so close to one another. But, could he see at night? The area is on a steep slope on crumbling earth prone to landslides, and there is no public light. What, should he hurt himself? I was adamant that was the sure way to eliminate any danger to my garden. Yes, if I alerted the authorities first and they did not respond in the way I wanted them to, and then hire a woodman it would be obvious I was involved in the execution of the job. So I phoned my friend. His daughter answered: "He is in his workshop right now, please call again at lunch time". I phoned again at 12:00 pm. The same voice on the phone: "He is not here, please call at 13:00".

"What about tonight, from what time can I find him in?" I enquired.

"Yes, after 19:30".

I gave up. There was something odd about that voice. Maybe it was not meant to be, maybe it was just wrong. I searched for the most effective felling technique for trees, twenty-thirty metres tall, and in that spot no way my friend could have worked in the secrecy of darkness. So my first idea was not implementable. The morning after my foiled attempt, I went to the garden, sat at the table reading but my mind was up into the Robinias foliage above. By now those trees had become my obsession as if a race against time had just begun and time was closing in on me. How can anyone feel so abandoned by society in 2023 when communication has never before been so much at the centre of human relationships? I wonder. But again people feel falsely empowered by the ability to express their opinion on Facebook, Twitter, Instagram, etc, etc, when all they do is chat. Yes, chat; one hundred years ago men used to gather in their private clubs and bars to gossip; women used to gather around the fire knitting and gossip; they did not change the world; the ones who temporarily overturned the rules, took to the streets, shouted their slogans, rallied and protested demanded their rights be legally recognized and upheld in the law. Yes, the law that people in power draft up and expect everyone else to respect but themselves. The law that changes as people's opinions, beliefs, values and framework of societal expectation or moral codes change. Law, fashion, rights and not many corresponding duties. Bottom line, I have a problem which is shared by my neighbours and I do not know what to do to obtain positive results; that is 2023 for you... Impulsively, my frustration mounting I switched on my phone and dialled the emergency number. Now I was ready to take them on, yes, with the spirit of a suffragette, I was determined to be listened to. The calling centre enquired about the nature of my request. "I need an urgent intervention by the fire brigade to assess the perilousness of a very tall tree on public soil".

They put me through to the police; I told them I needed the fire brigade; they obliged. I finally was able to talk to the authorities who were competent in the forestry field. If people call on them to save kittens from the top of trees and roofs, surely they would intervene by rushing to assess a tree of twenty metres in length whose trunk had fallen out of its base circumference and was leaning visibly to one side? Meaning it had an increased chance of falling at any time thus potentially wounding anyone on the public path below? They took down my description of the situation as I saw it and my deep concern about the possible consequences should they fail to intervene.

"We are certainly going to come and have a look, Madam".

"And when is that going to be?"

"Instantly!" they replied.

I could not believe it. Because I had just talked to someone who seemed to take me seriously, I started to feel a bit better. Soon I would be pouring out my soul face-to-face with other human beings. I always thought highly of the fire brigade as first line professionals getting involved in dire situations thus endangering their own lives in the process of either preserving or saving someone else's; they are contrasting figures compared with the pen-pushers wearing suits in the town hall with an appalling record of a pitiful reputation of layabouts. I was deeply aware my inner peace had been profoundly shattered by the fallen branch a few days before and I no longer thought of my garden as a sanctuary where to let go and forget about the terrible world around me. It seemed this very world was conniving against me setting up all sorts of impediments, menace and hazards to rob me of my sacrosanct peace of mind, my legitimate right to tranquility and intimate soul-searching. I needed help. I must trust the people around me even if hesitantly, circumspectly. So far my neighbours had proven to be friendly and instrumental to both my garden's and my well-being. I never expected them to be so forthcoming and helpful, but there! They pleasantly surprised me. And would I underestimate the importance of having good neighbours over the wall? You never know till you need them and I know how lucky I am. In fact the fallen branch of poor Plum tree was contributory in bringing us all together. Indeed I had never met the neighbours over the southern wall before; the fear of the unknown planted a seed in my heart and suspicion about whom they might be and what they might be like were shattered and replaced by trust and friendliness. I was safe in my fortress, save for these pernicious Acacia trees, still garrulous with the raspberries of the magpies. Wrapped up in my thoughts, I was shaken to attention by some nearing voices and quick, heavy footsteps. I opened my gate and, there were my saviours. They had arrived.

"Please, come into my garden and stand under the menacing branches and heavy canopies of the Robinias. Just get a feel for their might and potential destructive power; see the bole over there? The one nearest to the garden wall, just over the public path? It is not straight; it is leaning towards my garden, and the long, bendy, lateral branches, are almost reaching down to touch my vase on the pillar. And come over here, you see? This is the scar left over from a large branch that fell on my amphora three days ago. No one could have ever imagined it would snap, just like that! 'Snap!' under the beating fury of the last storm."

"OK, let's go out and assess the health of the tree", one of the men tells me.

We all walked as far as the wooded corner, a few steps along the path and they all convened to say that it was not an emergency. The trees were young, healthy, flexible with a deep root apparatus which anchored them solidly. (All Robinias have deep roots as opposed to conifers which have extensive but superficial rooting networks). The toppled acacias further back had fallen because being already dry and dead. Should the tree ever fall it would do so onto the wall so my garden would be spared the full impact and only the tip of the canopy would come through. So no worry about the trees, however, yes, the area was somewhat neglected, they observed, and definitely needed tidying up.

"All you have to do is to call into the town hall and request the intervention of their handymen and clear up the mess."

"But", I was quick to chip in, "what about the leaning tree? Can't you back my claim up by sending a report to the town hall?"

"You see, if we were to do that, we would have to seal off the entire area, including the access to your garden, till the problem is solved."

"I understand; many thanks for coming and for your advice. I am just very concerned." They all smiled at me and one of them gave me his phone number so I could send a copy of my identity card. So back to the drawing board for me. C'est la vie! However, the fire brigade had carried out a survey; they had logged my call, taken my details and made two photos of the trees and bramble jungle over the footpath spanning the two walls on each of its sides. Well, now armed with this first experience, I could commence my long journey into the labyrinth of public bureaucracy, meandering my way through the winding, dark tunnels of the Italian public administration. The hairs on my arms stand up on top of the goose pimples that such repulsive thoughts provoke. Yes, I took action towards the course I believed in and psychologically, at least, I found it quite liberating, notwithstanding the result. Encouraged by the sense of empowerment, I decided to go further in my quest for justice on behalf of my beloved garden and wrote a short and to the point letter with a request for an urgent assessment and subsequent intervention to the technical department of the local town hall. Of course, I remembered to mention I had already been visited by the fire brigade who had suggested I had the area cleared by the town hall as it lay in a state of evident neglect. I sent my letter by email accompanied by four photos of the trees from inside my garden and from the path, addressed to a specific person whom is responsible for maintaining both the public land and forest. Excellent, I felt even better now. I would allow one week and then I would call upon the manager in his office in person. Never allow your anxiety, negative emotions and fear to build up inside you. Have a built-in release valve to deflate the pressure and to keep enjoying what it is here now and not be concerned with what could disappear tomorrow.

The clock strikes 11:00, the sound of the bells diffuses into my chest like fluid osmosis and expands inside my body, focusing my attention on my otherwise discounted and taken for granted anatomical structures, my rib cage, my stomach, my heart and it circulates before being dissipated, absorbed by my blood and eventually to be breathed out, soundless.

I can hear voices in the alleyway; they are getting closer, more and more. They have stopped in front of my gate. They are standing behind it. It must be them; it is them, my guests. I have been waiting for them for three hours and when I last saw them it was last year. I hardly know them; I do not know them whatsoever, in fact. They are strangers to me as much as I am a stranger to them, but I feel I have known them all my life, I trust them and am looking forward to welcoming them. Rosco has risen his head, ears pricked with curiosity more than alarm, a tell tale sign of no dog presence in the alleyway. Suddenly, I am seized with panic; is everything looking at its best in my garden? A quick scan reveals a few long blades of grass that have escaped my attention while weeding my borders earlier on. Why am I worried? Grass, glorious grass, what would we do without it? It is the most common green occurrence of a most varied colour ranging from dark, to light to variegated. Let's look at the structure of the long blades, the central vein, the different textures, species, some even bloom at certain times of the year. Grass is part of the natural world's wonders and must be loved and welcomed, though in moderation, in my garden. So no, I am not going to pluck those two blades by the Lavender bush, they blend in beautifully. Disappointment, surprise, praise, doubtfulness; what feelings will my garden elicit? My guests' perception plays a big part in their judgement. In a way I am so glad I did not send them any photo of my work in progress or of some finished project, because a picture might have given them the false impression. How many times our expectations are raised at the sight of a holiday resort, a must-have garment, a hair do viewed on the internet only to be disheartened when in contact with the object of our desire? Reality always hits us differently from a well-presented or even airbrushed photo, the concept of beauty and desirability is greatly altered by the modern tricks of visual impact. One such example is the estate agents' advertisements of premises to either rent or buy with brilliantly wide-angled photographed rooms, later improved with photo shop accompanied by equally impressively eloquent and detailed descriptions. However, during a personal viewing of the property, the reality turns out to be often a far cry from the website promises and a disappointment in the potential client can be read on the facial expression, hesitancy and a general state of bewilderment! Truth of the matter is we all create a mental picture of what we like to see or have and only the truth will or will not match our forecast. Of course, we should always be willing to compromise and our brain can help us adjust our prediction so as to lead us to accepting a modified initial framework of reference. However, when our mental processes are interfered with by external stimuli such as videos, photos, sketches, verbal advertisements, our perception of what we are after is altered to a certain extent; it greatly depends on the sensibilities of each individual, naturally. When influenced by the external world we lose our personal ability to scrutinize; we relinquish our freedom to judge and discern and fall foul to other people's desires and aspirations. In other words we cease to exist as people true to ourselves, we lose our authenticity. In my case, my guests have not been bamboozled into any flattering assumption and the only image of the garden they hold is from their memory of an empty space where grass, briars and a large lavender bush grew. The difference between then and now is stark, that is for sure. Their degree of appreciation will be derived from their aesthetic values and believes. It is not my vanity that dictates my thoughts but my need to oblige, to please, to show gratefulness to such an unique and rare family.

Following a few verbal exchanges, a female voice calls out my name: "Della, are you in? We are here."

I spring from my chair, the dog in toe and all my worries, considerations, elucubrations disappear, get reabsorbed into my mind like water previously wrung out of a sponge gets sucked back up into the same after the grip on the latter has been released. I stretch my arm towards the gate, get hold of two iron bars and with one firm movement I swing the gate open.

"Come in, come in!" I exhort my guests, four of them and quite eager to step inside.

"I welcome you into my magical garden", I cry with delight and utmost excitement.

The first to appear is my benefactor's daughter. We only met last year in October at the notary's. I liked her straight away and back then we took the decision to be on friendly terms. I cannot remember her at all. Her hair seems different, the colour, the do, the length? And she is thinner than I recollect. Perhaps her clothes were thicker; it was autumn after all. The one thing that strikes me, though, is her large, warm smile which opened my heart that October day. She greets me with fervour and we fall into each other's embrace. How wonderful the real person is; much better than that my brain has managed to elaborate over time. Her kind and friendly personality gushes with happiness and her mind is as transparent as the pool of a mountain brook. My whole being senses the positive vibes and I am filled with positive feelings as a consequence. Immediately behind her is my benefactress, Maria. We exchange a warm, heartfelt hug and look in to each other's eyes, hers as clear and as deep as the sky above, as I welcome her into not mine but our garden and once again I thank her profusely for her generosity. I look at her and the old delicate frame of her body does not do any justice to this lady's strong, healthy character and her beautiful 'Joy de vivre'. I can detect a hint of exasperation coming from Maria whose biological age is a total mismatch between what she looks like and her young, crisp and vital personality. My mind cannot help wondering how I would be feeling trapped inside an older body still young at heart and willing to do so much more with my life. A sentiment of frustration bubbles up and I am filled with compassion and admiration for this extraordinary person who was able to see through me and read my heart like the pages of an open book, and moreover, just in a matter of minutes. She trusted me, and the past is history as the saying goes. The two men follow, Maria's son in law and her adult grandson. I move to one side and let them take the whole garden in. They look amazed, stunned, even emotional. They start moving around noticing the design, the plants arrangement, furniture, little objects, artifacts, that sprang from instant ideas with association of previous finds in the guise of stones, twigs, shells and more. My guests' eyes beam, they are wide-open and they point out the features they find so appealing. Maria's eyes well and I really feel touched. It is a success; I did it, I managed to turn around a piece of wasteland and make it into a beautiful, English garden. I am so very happy, so grateful that their gesture has triumphed into an accomplished dream, not just for me but for them, too. I stand in awe of my hard work and of how Nature seems to have met my desires half way by expressing itself through its living, magical world within these ancient walls.

"How creative you are; your creativity is amazing, look at that illusion! As soon as I saw it I wondered how on earth you had managed to open a window into the neighbours' wall. The tortoises made of rocks and their naturally carved head, really!"

"Yes, I spotted this expressive stone while walking along the path just below the garden, and I thought it resembled a tortoise's head."

"Of course, you have an artistic eye, you can distinguish what we cannot even see."

They stop at every corner finding new features to enjoy. I point out the statuette of Saint Fiacre and immediately, Maria's son-in-law knows who he is and what he represents.

"Prometheus, yes", Maria's daughter cries out, "I remember his name from my studies of Greek mythology."

They touch all the herbs, smell their fingers and boast their knowledge with one another.

"This is an educational trail!" says on of them.

"I would like to bring to your attention that I have recycled as much material as possible from the heap that was standing in the south-eastern corner of the garden; there was a lot of refuse buried there and amongst all the items that I found were the terracotta sherds from broken floor tiles, which I used by leaning them against the wall to provide a safe haven for the little inhabitants of the garden. At the end of the day I owe it to them since they were living here before I took possession of the land, in fact I am a guest in their home."

Everybody looks at me in acknowledgement of my statement. If they could just witness the brilliant job the Rufus slugs carry out along the eastern and southern borders as diligent composters, chomping on all the fallen plums and leaves that would otherwise decompose and give off a foul smell that attracts wasps and flies and other unwanted carrions. The slugs are the real gardeners here keeping all perishable material and accumulating debris in check. Once recovered from their surprise the four of them congratulate me; they commend me on my creativity,

173

operosity, but above all my love and respect for this sliver of land. I can wait no more and am poised to ask the very question that has been gnawing at my mind since acquiring the plot. Guess work has been ongoing but knowing the workings of the human conscience, everything one ponders too much, for too long, and too often, gets bigger and bigger and becomes bedecked with all sorts of fantasies that serve the purpose to meet with our prospectives. So now it is the right time to whittle down any self-formed conjectures and ask a direct question, why did you sell me the plot if you seem so keen on it? But no sooner had I formulated the question in my mind than Maria speaks up, her mouth quivering:

"I remember, you know, I remember very well the day I met you in my kitchen; your words are still ringing in my ears, 'even if we do not manage to wrap up this deal, I am keen on pursuing a friendship'; then I knew you were the right person. I felt it in my heart."

Her daughter buts in, keen to let me know: "Yes, yes, the same day Mother called me in Milan to tell me she had come by a suitable candidate to take over the garden. She told me how lovely a person you came across as and what an infectious enthusiasm burst out of your words and eyes. I was looking forward to meeting you and we only did it once, at the notary's to sign the deed of sale, remember?"

Maria continues, "We only tried to sell the garden once many years back, but the prospective buyers said it cost too much, not our proposed selling price but the notary's fees. Then, we were very disappointed but did not search for anyone else to sell the plot. It stayed with us all this time till you came along. We planted hydrangeas, a huge rosemary bush; the lavender was my daughter's. At first we were very excited to have bought the house we had been renting for many years over the summer holidays and even more so, because it had a small garden attached to it. Little did we know then that because we were coming but once or twice a year for a few weeks only, the garden became overgrown soon and fast with brambles encroaching onto the lawn, the grass getting out of hand; the plants suffering through neglect and the neighbouring cats using the plot as an habitual place to relieve themselves. We suffered to witness the disrepair and rapid deterioration our beloved plot fell into during our prolonged absence. We could do nothing to take care of it and Nature took over as it does when no one is there to tame it. So after the past few years we had resorted to having the grass cut down regularly and the briars kept in check with a strimmer by a local, trusted handyman. However, it was never the right solution for the garden. We had even thought of buying a gazebo, a table, some chairs at some point, but to what avail? We were never here to enjoy it. The day I met you I knew you were able to make the most of it, because of your geographical vicinity and your forthcoming good intentions. Thank you."

"Oh no, thank you again for your unselfishness and open mindedness. Most people would rather have left the garden perish than giving it away to make someone else happy. You put the well-being of your garden first thus making me happy," I am eager to let Maria know, "and that is laudable. In fact I believe gardens should bring people together not set them apart. You basically gifted this garden to me because of the expenses you faced in order to draft the proxy documents which you had to sign while in hospital before a notary in Milan. That must have cost you something. Then the low price you set for my purchase, the lowest permissible by law, in fact, which was even queried by the notary himself, who feared the reaction by the land registry officials, who may have deemed the price to be too low for a legal sale. So, as a matter of fact you almost gave me your garden for free, as you made no profit whatsoever. That I know for sure!" I state with conviction.

"Yes, some people would have speculated on it; we were keen on the garden to end up in safe hands first and foremost."

We smile and hug again. Now we all know the reason why this garden is magic, it was a token of love and was instrumental in sealing our budding friendship. The accidental, loving relationship between two families who, a few minutes before the garden brought us together, knew absolutely nothing of one another's existence. The affinity we are discovering amongst ourselves, the love for Nature, art, to name but a few interests, is extremely rare amongst strangers who chance to meet for the first time. Maria's grand-son seems to be a sensitive just like I am and stares at me in approval when I say I felt the garden call me in when I first walked by it and caught a glimpse of it through the iron bars of the gate. It vibrated positively, it stirred something inside me like no other place ever did before. I felt it had been waiting for me to discover it and what happened next I attribute to good karma.

Now that the truth behind the sale has finally been revealed I look at this garden with deep reverence for the benevolent power it unleashed to bring us all together, to get to know one another and to forge a relationship which, with time may prove indissoluble. I dare say that I just wish we were a family and Maria is quick to reply she feels as if we were because of the truly honest and good feelings that run through us. Blood relations are not always good for the heart and real friends are always there for you because, 'love is stronger than blood.' How very true. The saying, 'blood is thicker than water' never held true for me, at least not all the times as one may delude oneself into idealistic expectations from family members only to be let down and be supported by real friends instead. There you go! Expectations again! What Maria is preaching is what she is actually doing, by implementing the same, 'the blood of the covenant is thicker than the water of the womb'. Indeed, more often than not, the bonds we choose are more significant and impact our lives more strongly than the bonds with our relatives. I feel so at ease in the presence of these people who understand me perfectly, down to my quirky tendencies or at least what I thought were only within my quirky remit till Maria's daughter, out of the blue tells me she loves visiting graveyards especially, old, forlorn tombs, the one in the local cemetery she feels the most attracted to. That's one of the first things she does when she comes here on holiday.

"I normally visit an old lady whose photo is antique, she is all by herself and I keep her some company".

"I think I know where she is buried; she is the lady with the oval black and white picture with her head wrapped in a shawl, her eyes closed..." I attempt.

"Yes, yes, that's the one!" Maria's daughter confirms without hesitation.

How can two perfect strangers feel pity for whom they deem to be a lonely and forgotten, old, deceased lady in the local cemetery? Is this a coincidence? If so, it is really weird. My life is jam-packed with fortuitous coincidences and this garden is one of them. Coincidences or universal law of good and evil of 'what goes round comes round'. Of the twelve magical laws that govern the universe, the one that stands in our encounter is the law of Divine Oneness. It is true our deep awareness of feelings, beliefs and actions, take shape through repetitive patterns in our life and that we gain insight into who we are as part of the connection with the entire universe. That universe is our garden in this case and through it we found one another, with a similar approach to life, interests, ideology and attitudes. Our garden is a beloved pet, a live unit made up of many other living units, whose previous owners, with much regret waited for the right people to give it up for adoption. Of course the garden still belongs to them spiritually, as much as it belongs to me because even if separate, we are one. Maria sits down in one of the chairs, exhausted more through emotional overload than physical exertion. We keep chatting, discussing this feature and that feature; the effort and work I had to put into it, how long it took me to accomplish everything. Now it is time for them to share the design and step-by-step transformation of our pet garden, Little HighGrove. I suggest we share my link of the photographic album which gets regular updates through the seasons, as I have been immortalizing every aspect of my paradise since the very day I acquired it on October 4th, 2022. They accept eagerly so I add Maria's and her daughter's names to my list of private guests to which only I and my husband belong. My friends are the only privileged people to partake in the privacy of our garden whose struggles, successes and virtues must be appreciated with insight and compassion, two gifts my friends are endowed with. I wonder how many of the locally abandoned gardens would benefit from a loving make over but the latter would be the outcome of their owners' selfless behaviour. Such behaviour they are incapable of and the neglect, disrepair and general dereliction one comes across while walking along the paths that coast all of the little plots is heartbreaking and much a reflection of human self-destructive nature by allowing the deterioration of the environment around them. While we talk, I cast an eye on Maria, who, very quietly is observing, contemplating and absorbing her garden; what she can see is the outcome of her trust, good-heartedness and utter generosity. She must be feeling satisfied with her deed and her heart must now be at peace knowing the garden is well looked after and, after all, still there for her to enjoy when we come together within its magic precincts.

Half the hour past 11:00 has tolled by the church bell, the same bell that has marked the passing of time throughout this morning, this memorable, very special morning, the only factor that has tidied me to my presence existential reality, while the rhythm in between the resonant peels has been absorbed by my inner voice, sensations, feelings, hopes, preoccupations, memories and faith, faith in the Universe.

"Oh, we must go now, we have guests for lunch. So kind of you to invite us and we strongly commend you on all we have seen. We could not have hoped for anything better than this."

We kiss, hug and promise to keep in touch. We all know we want to see one another again and again in the future and to get to know one another more in depth. Before too long I will be able to visit their house to show them my garden sketchbook, my watercolour tables for the design of the garden outline, my garden journals and my latest book about the garden which I am delighting in penning right now. Yes, this very book which has been inspired by the faithful encounter with my new special friends through the love for a garden. That very kitchen where Maria and I exchanged the first words, the first looks and feelings which sealed our shared dream, the well-being of the garden. I see them out of the narrow gate; before disappearing down the alleyway they all turn round and smile at me, happy with what they have witnessed, surely beyond any construed wild expectation but truly capable of making a clear comparison with the plot they relinquished and the garden they have just enjoyed.

What a joy, what a relief! I sit down in my chair again and my perception of the garden has completely changed, filtered through my guests' comments and facial expression. All my doubts, fears, obsessive behaviours have dissipated, they have dissolved into the air just like the brazen tolling of the bells from the church tower. All that I am left to contemplate with a light and contented heart is the slow pace of Nature in the plants, the small organisms, the cracks in the walls, the breeze and the peaceful beating of my heart inside my chest.

One garden, one friendship, one life, all celebrated in one book; I think this is one story of the essence as a human being well worth writing and I hope worth reading, too, through the lines to capture the true meaning of our existence as specs of energy-charged dust in the vast Universe in which we exist and which throbs inside each of us here on Earth. I am HAPPY, a feeling that has a fleeting, ephemeral, fugacious nature but on this occasion the sensation is different; it displays a more substantial reason which encapsulates the new reality that is shaping my perception: my new friends understand me.

Yes, they do; they are capable of discerning the reasons behind my thoughts and actions. I feel I can truly communicate my needs and hopes to them and be appreciated. This garden is the living link between us, the umbilical cord that nourishes us and allows us to thrive. But then how can anyone be capable of true happiness this day and age with a war raging on in Ukraine at the hands of the Russian government moved by ancient, outdated sentiments of imperial pride (which never died down since the Stalin era) through the repossession of lands that had obtained their independence and only hope for peace and prosperity but won't give up their hard earned freedom and democracy; a viral pandemic that turned the world upside down for two years and keeps rearing its ugly head through variants of the original virus, immune to the current available vaccines. The climate crisis which is nothing more than a sudden wake up call through weather extremes which were predicted, researched by world-renowned scientists sixty odd years ago; and last but not least the cost of living crisis with unemployment, mental illness rampant amongst the new generation, mass migrations from war and famine-torn countries and social unrest as corollaries to this wretched human existence which is the ultimate outcome of all the afore-mentioned man-made and man-facilitated disasters. There isn't much to smile about, I rationally reckon. But in spite of the troubled times we are living through, I cannot help being happy. Am I delusional? If I were sad, disgruntled, somber, critical, paranoid and ultimately, just like many people I pass by every day in the street, tell me, what difference would I make to the plight we all face? The answer is, NONE! So, I am determined to ride on the wings of happiness, like the wings of a butterfly, on the jump of a cricket, the plunge of a swallow in the deep, blue sky, the tumble of a raindrop, the swirling circles of a falling leaf. Yes, that short-lived moment of utter mental and physical well-being, that unique personal experience of complete abandonment, indescribable, rapturous instant in which in spite of everything, I allow myself to exult, to explode with a megaton power of positive energy, showering down with confetti, rose petals, Jasmine flowers that fall on me fresh as morning dew, as the wave of a woodland brook, as the foot of a snail. Because, tell me, has there been a single moment when within this world there is no suffering whatsoever, no hunger, no hatred, no betrayal, physical or psychological violence, to give me licence, to allow me to be truly happy with no remorse? The answer is no! Therefore, if I want to be happy, then I MUST, and the time is now.

Time, that illusory, human invention...

TIME

How elusive yet so tangible
The there and then
The here and now
Mixing, swapping, overlapping in
                    a row.
Chase Time up, time catches up
                    with me
It's cat and mouse game, I do not feel
                    free
Time paces my life, decisions
Accomplished objectives, dreams and
                    more...
Time is needed, I have to go.
Days, months, years, Time we
                    measure
But when Time runs out we reach our
                    tether.
How can the infinite nature of Time
                    run out?
Barriers we impose, set free the
                    Spout.
Stop
Make
Lose
Spare   Time

Make hay while the sun shines.
Time and man - no friendship
                    sought

Camaraderie less than nought.
Saving Time makes no one any
                         richer
Time elapses, and that is the
                         feature.
Stop pretending and live today
'cause Time is in your hands, act
And it will obey.
Do not give Time to Time,
Seize your chance with prompt
                         bravery
And kiss goodbye the Time's
                         slavery.
(Della Livorno)

Happiness is but a fleeting moment which blends into contentment and peace of mind, gratefulness for that amazing feeling that regardless of all the darkness around us, regales us the strength to carry on and discover day by day the simplicity of life in the translucence of a leaf, the diaphanous transparency of a libellula's wings...

Soon autumn will breathe its entrance into my garden and the trees surrounding it will wrap their golden and crimson garments around its neck, at its feet and on the crowns of my plants, decorating them with multicoloured baubles, a festival of lights, an automnal Christmas sight.

LEAVES

Leaves, beautiful leaves,
falling leaves,
autumn with its known cape
        and cool fingers
in the woods lingers.

Day after day, the breeze elegant leaves
                rustles
as from the boughs leaves hang in
            cluttered hustles.

A whip of wind then some leaves
              snatches
of hurricane fury its strength
              matches.

The fall soon begins; the leaves rise first
on the air waves that through the
              stillness burst.

They twirl, they whirl a pirouette
They dance, enduring a
            fleeting stance...

Of yellow, copper red and
              streaks of green.
The canvass of the sky is painted
              akin.

Every leaf belongs to Heaven and
            beyond

Searching for the magic wand.

Alas! Life is no more and to the earth
the leaves go afore.

Waving, sumersaulting, quivering
        with fear
They feel the earth approach near.

With a thump, jolt or smooth
        touch down
Leaves collect on the soil brown.

A bright, soft carpet of cellulose
lays at the foot of trees bygone
        umbrose.

Reminiscent of vibrant life, vigour,
      energy, pretence.
In summer days so intense...

Leaves to soil, humous to life
Strength from death will triumph
        sure,
On new shoots boughs adore.

Fall, fall moribund leaves,
      your time
        is up,
no brethren sap can wake your nap.

Sleep, sleep on virgin earth
till spring will bustle birth.

        (Della Livorno)

I raise my eyes skyward and like the scales of a fish flashing silver in the oozing sunshine, so the high noon light shows through the green, wavy sea above. The threat of an imminent disaster now dispelled by my positive frame of mind, the Acacia trees seem to smile, winking yellow and spotted brown through the thick fringe of their canopies. My peace of mind has been restored, my soul healed and my hope rekindled. It is time to be happy again.

I look through my magic looking glass and what I see are my sparkling eyes and my delightful smile staring back at me from a beautiful garden beyond.

You see, "*The secret, Alice, is to surround yourself with people who make your heart smile. It is then, only then, that you will find Wonderland.*"

(Lewis Carroll)

Now I know, deep inside my heart I have found my Wonderland, at last.

EPILOGUE

It is five months since that July morning when my guests and I consolidated our friendship by celebrating our beloved garden's success and its enchanting story.

Back then, it was a hot, summer morning, imbued with the most vibrant of colours, scents and sounds. Today, I am standing in the same garden, deep in the slumber of winter, almost floating in the air, as the rich, luxuriant canopies, of the overhanging neighbouring trees have long parted with their leafy branches, which now gnarled and geriatric, agitate their bare, scrawny digits in the wind against a leaden sky. There is a window onto the mountains where the Robinia trees used to conceal the view, not because of lack of foliage, but because the menacing trees, now dead and mutilated, lie horizontally, littering the steep slope where they once stood, threateningly leaning over onto the garden, bent by the stormy gales. They have fallen victim to their decrepitude before their time at the hands of an experienced woodman who, in an act of deep friendship, put his skills to the service of the Spirit of the Place and, in so doing assured the long-term well-being and incolumity of my precious paradise. The sweet sound of chainsaws reverberated in the valley, one December dawn, when my friend and his son masterly felled four of those scraggy giants that in a tempest (a phenomenon now more frequently experienced without warning) might have broken off or become uprooted thus crashing full body onto my garden.

Their chopped trunks lie scattered on the undergrowth littered with a mulch of crumpled leaves and winged seeds, their scaly bark grooved with woody strands of Ivy whose dark green foliage, symbol of everlasting life, now cling on in a mere mockery. The thinner boughs piled up by the footpath; the forest of brambles that engulfed them, severed and thrown further down the incline. The ensuing clearing is like a breath of fresh air which will allow me to sleep tight in any weather. Now, in the nights to come, a wider stretch of sky above will be twinkling more readily and on moonlit evenings, the opalescent, silvery, sailing spaceship will illuminate the top of the mountain, maybe covered in a soft, white blanket of translucent snow to reflect the heavens above. On the other hand, the sun now free to show its brilliance directly from the open sky, will kiss my garden on its forehead with a profusion of inflorescences and thicker vegetation.

The potential threat now gone, I once again, feel at peace with Nature and can enjoy my garden in all seasons to come.

"Your days are numbered. Use them to throw open the windows of your soul to the sun.
If you do not, the sun will soon set, and you with it."

Marcus Aurelius   890 BC

THE
END

one summer morning in my garden

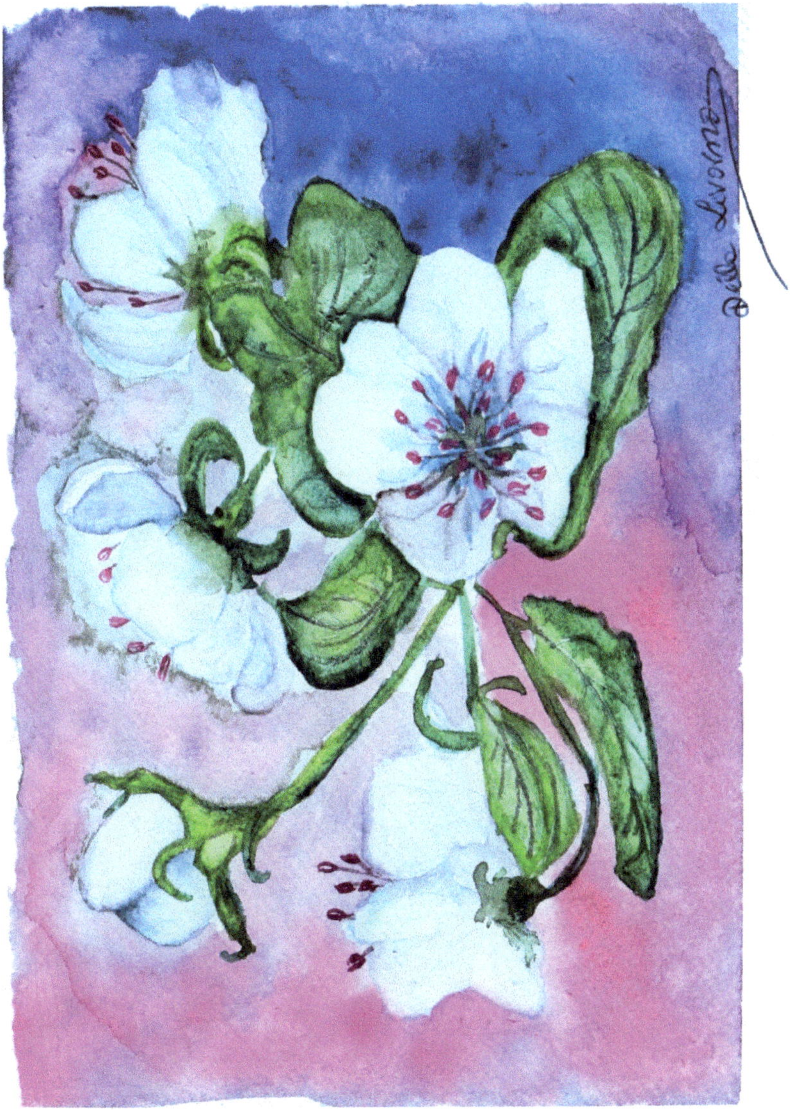

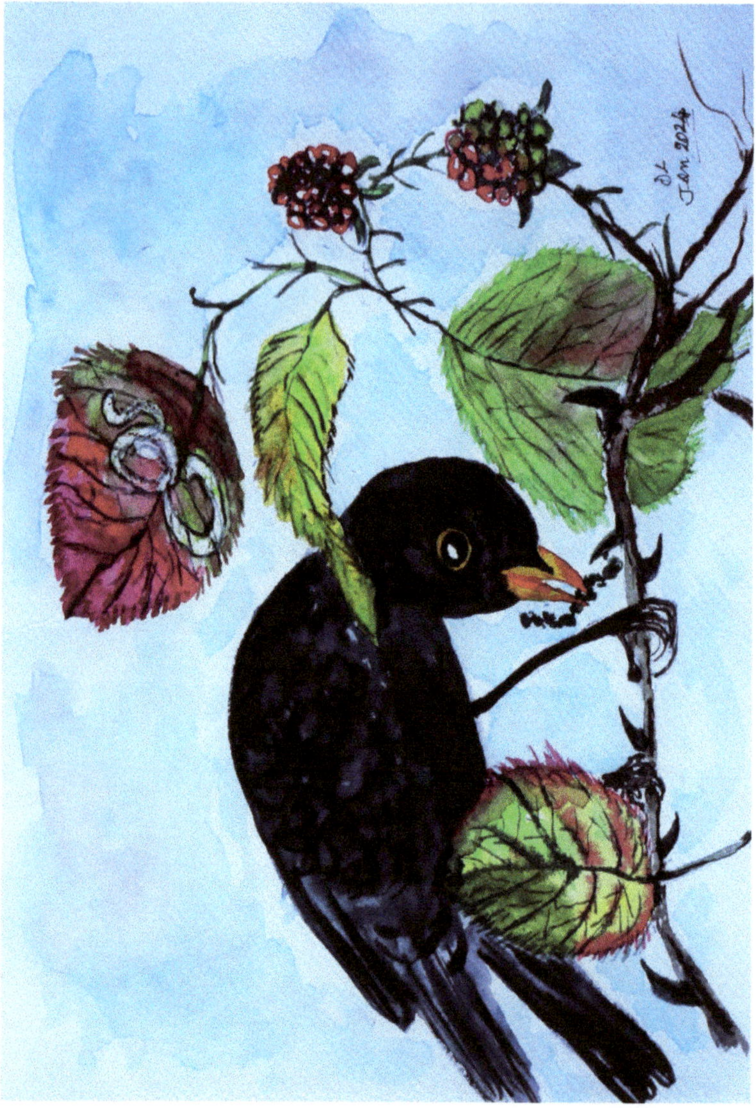
Jan 2024

Green Man   Genius Loci   The Spirit of The Place

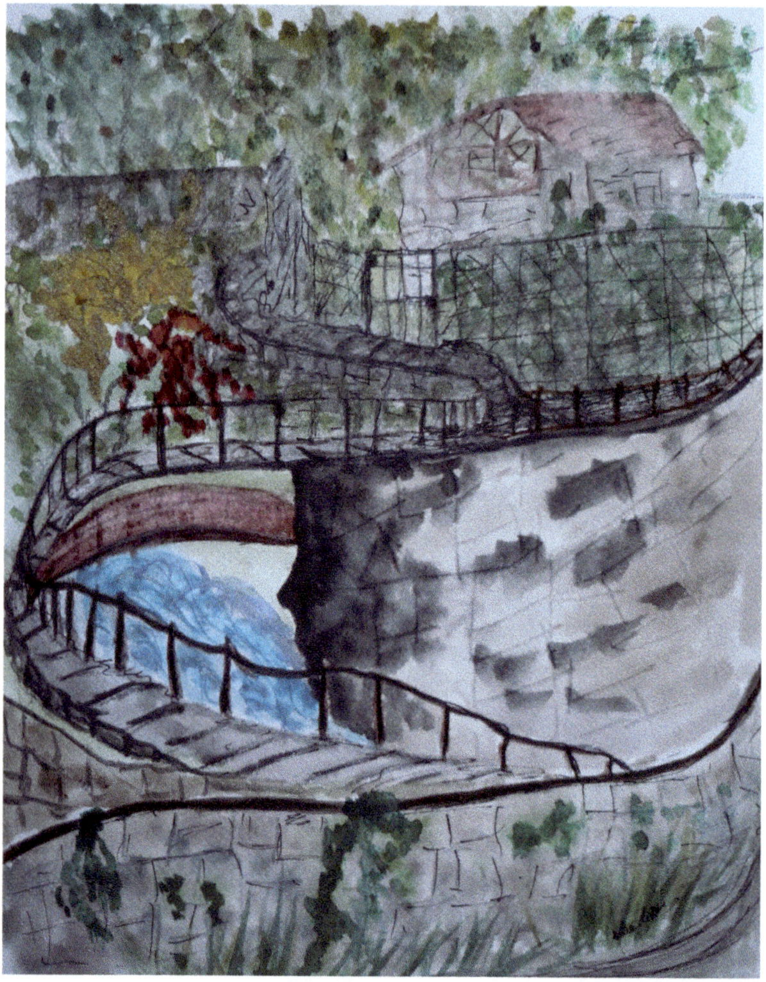

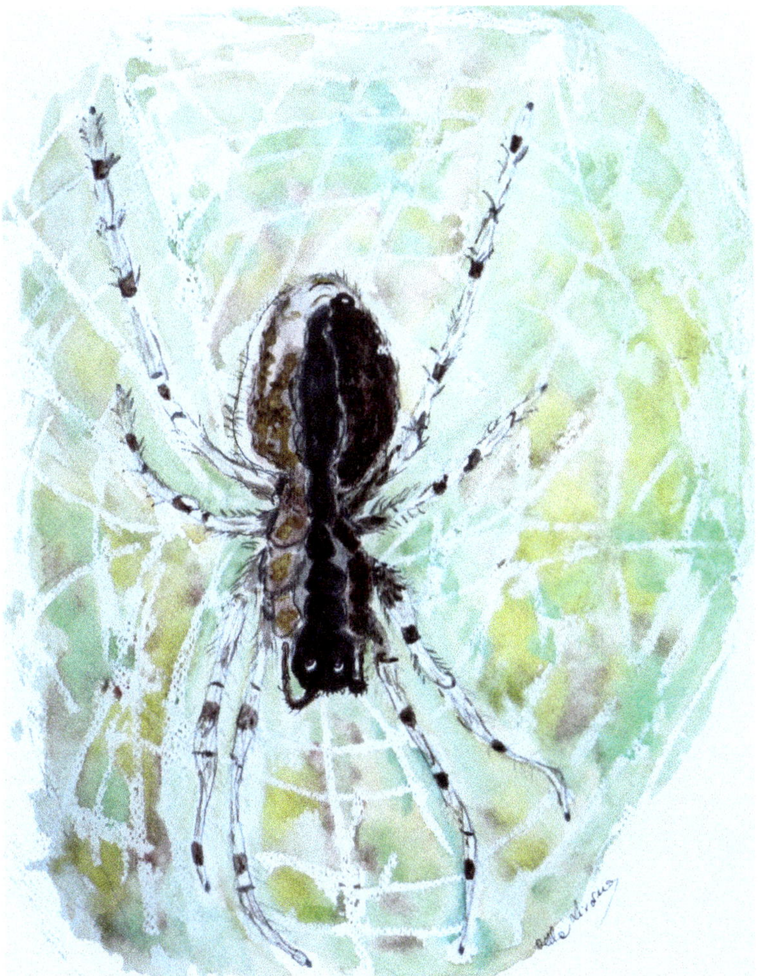

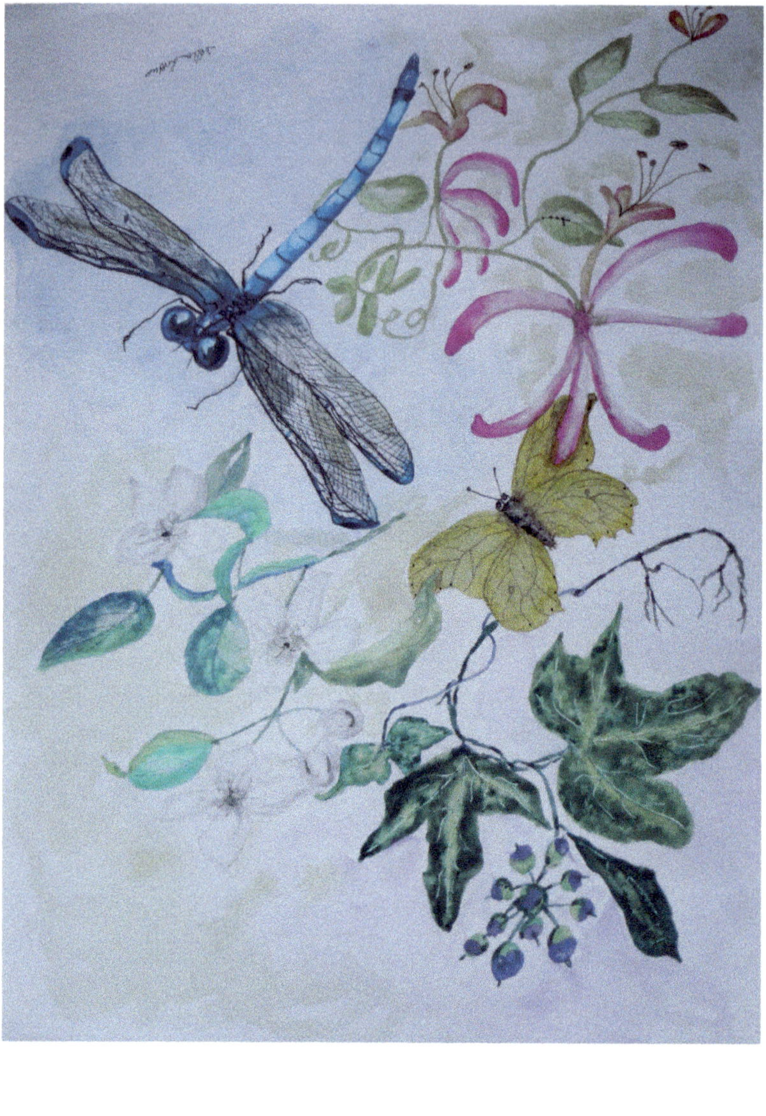

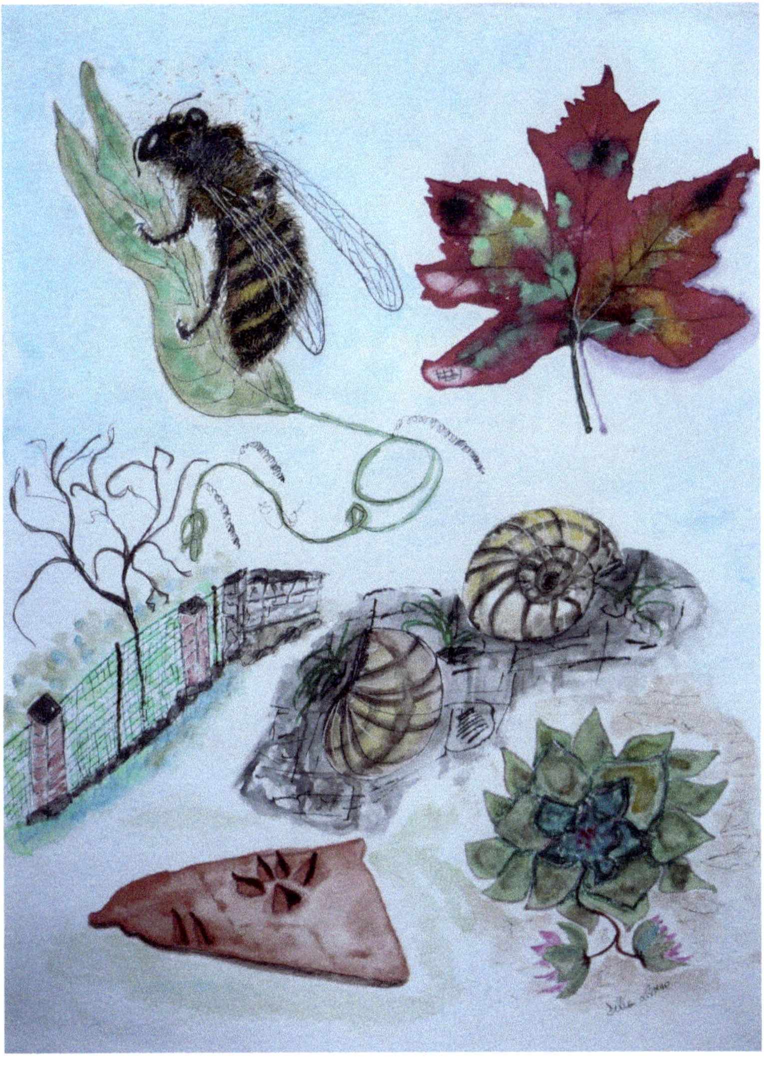

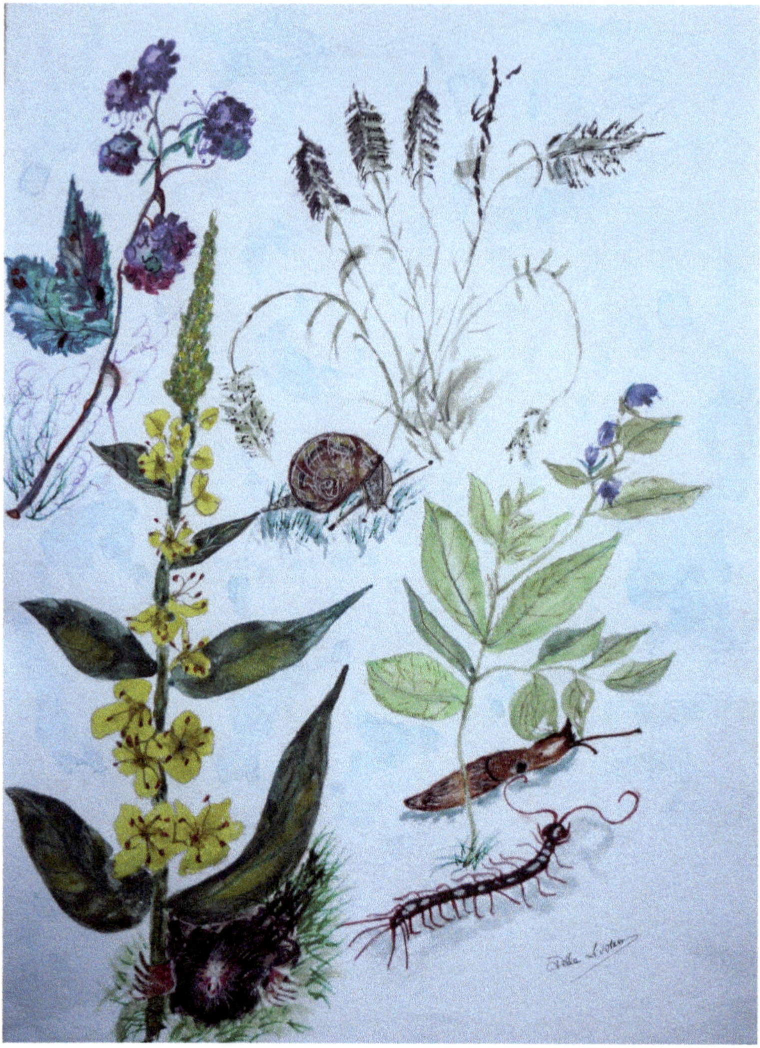

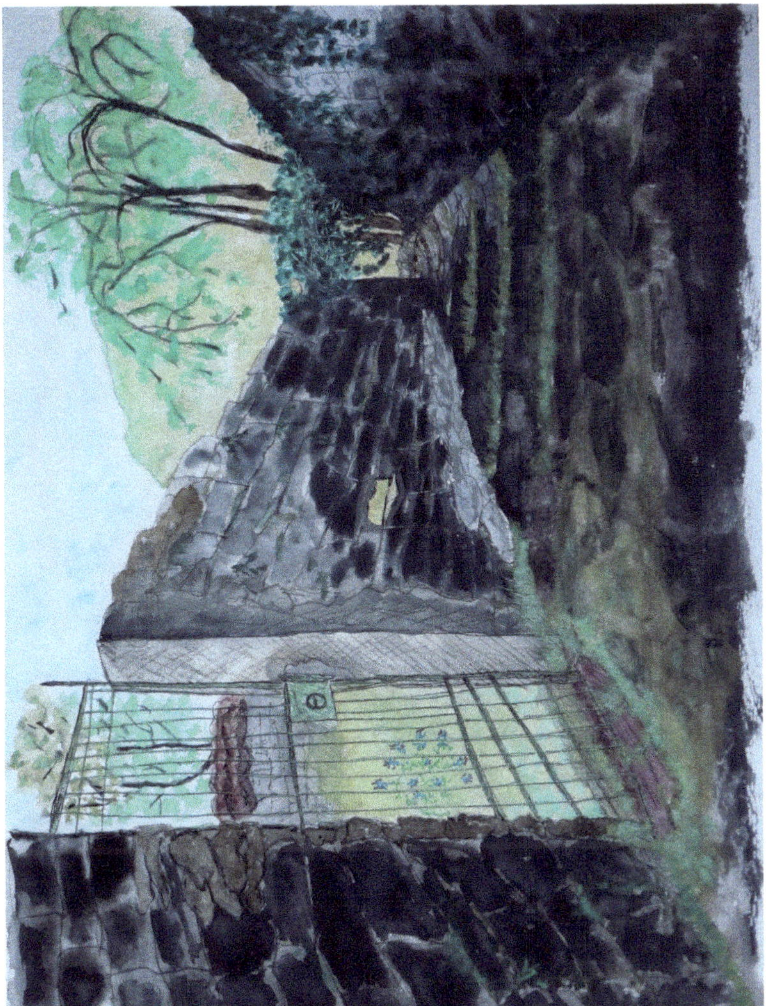

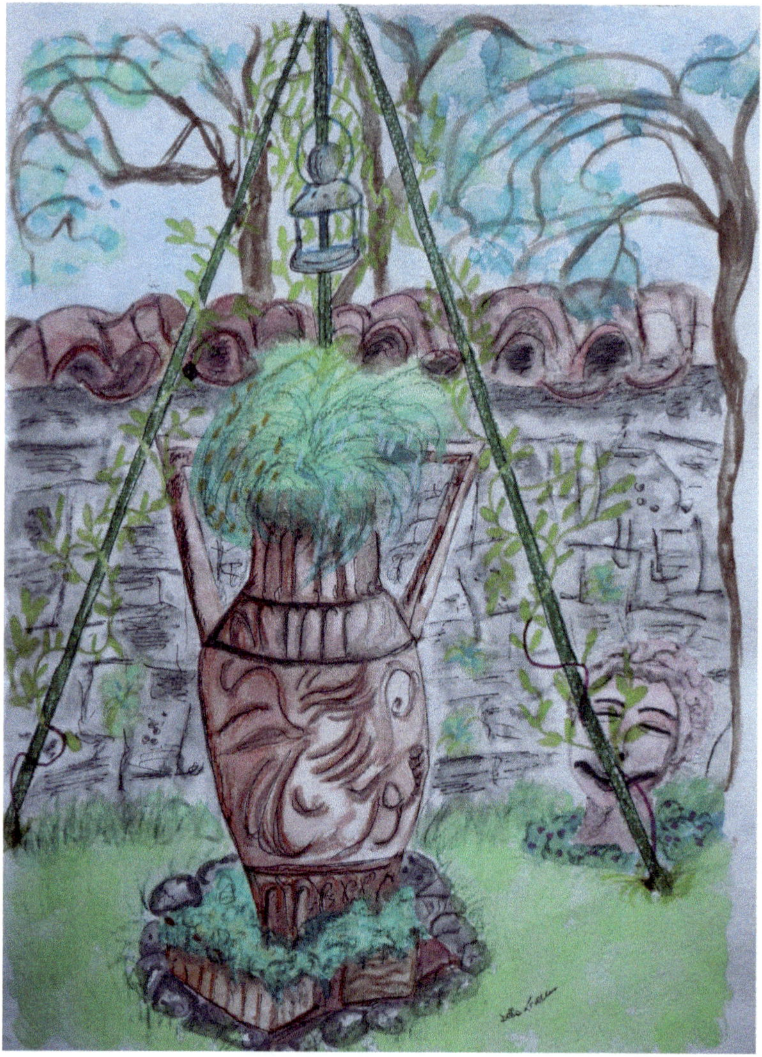

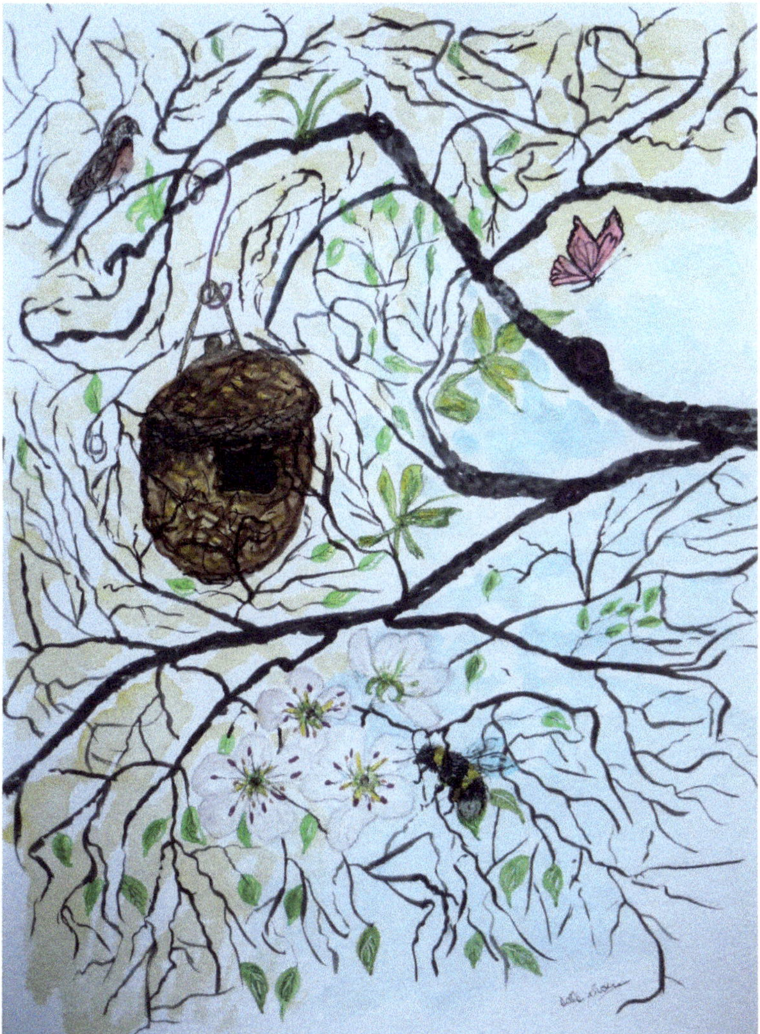

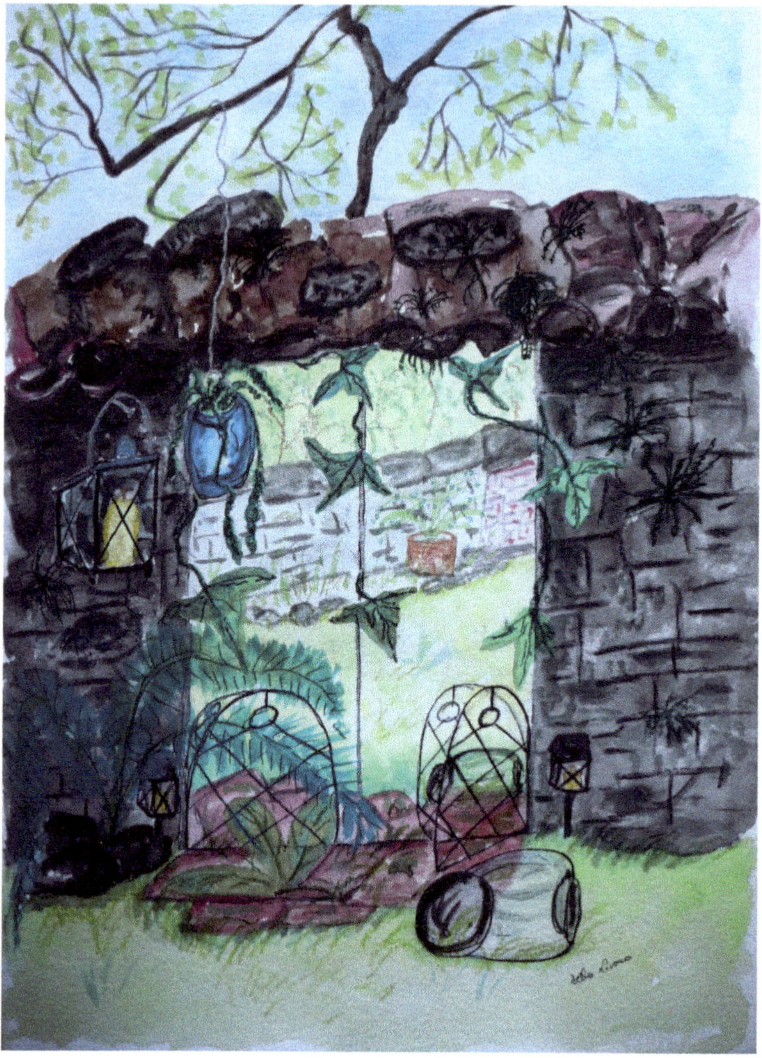

207

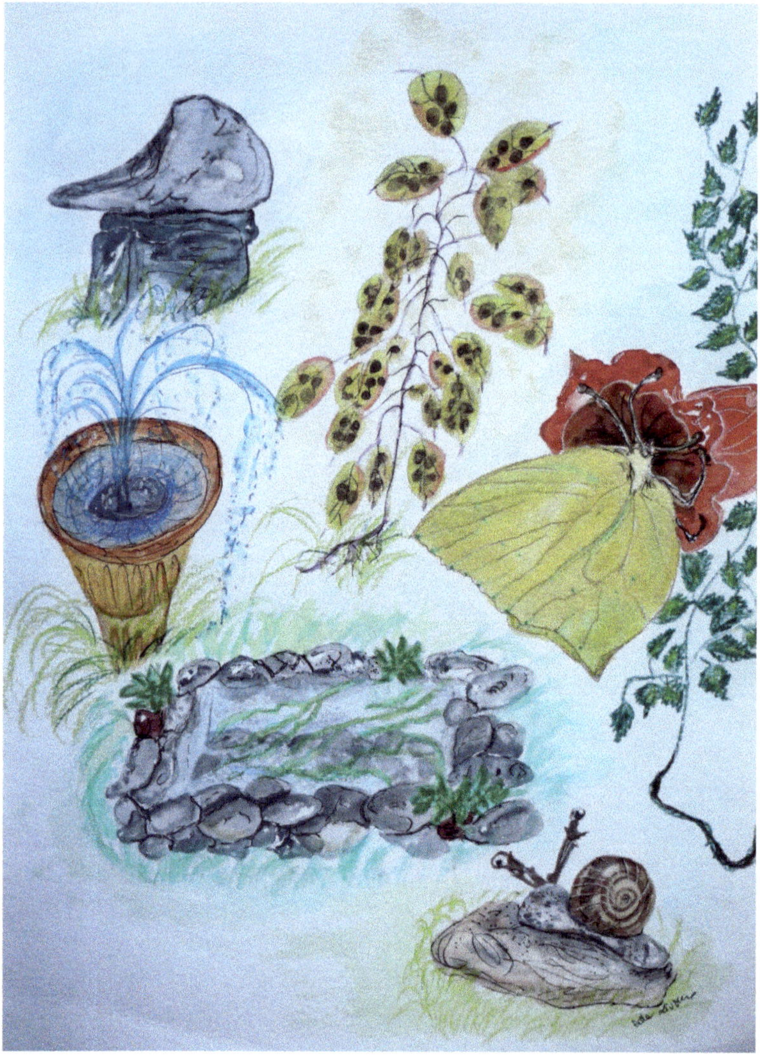

209

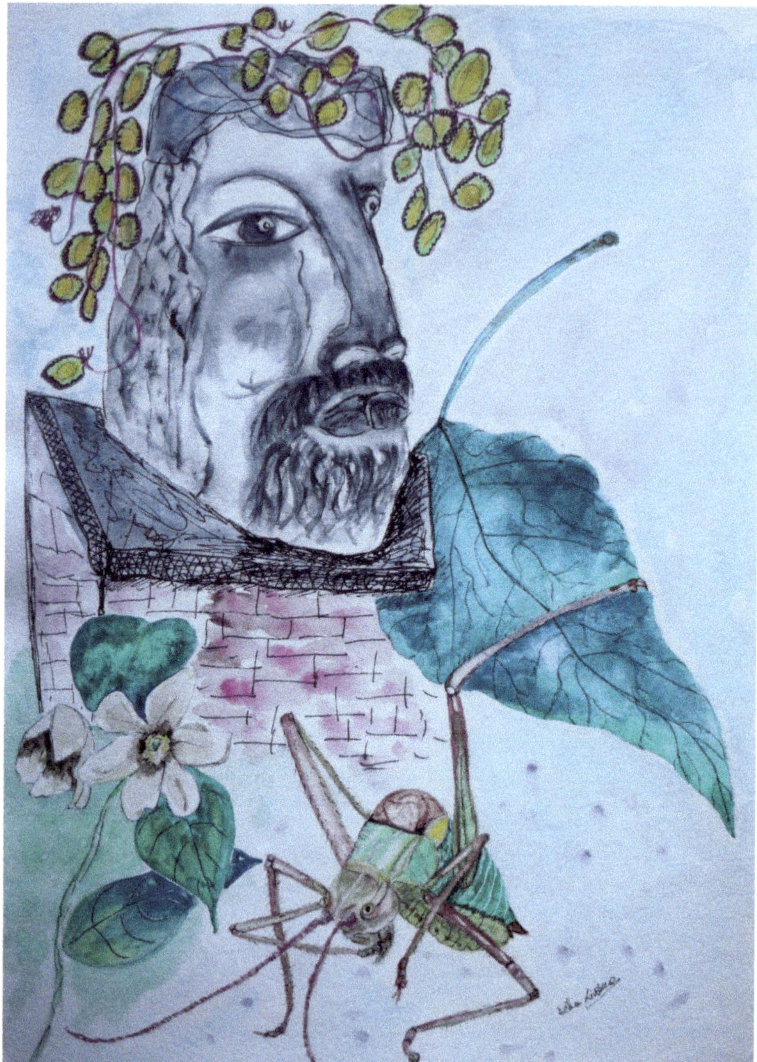

GRYLLUS CAMPESTRIS

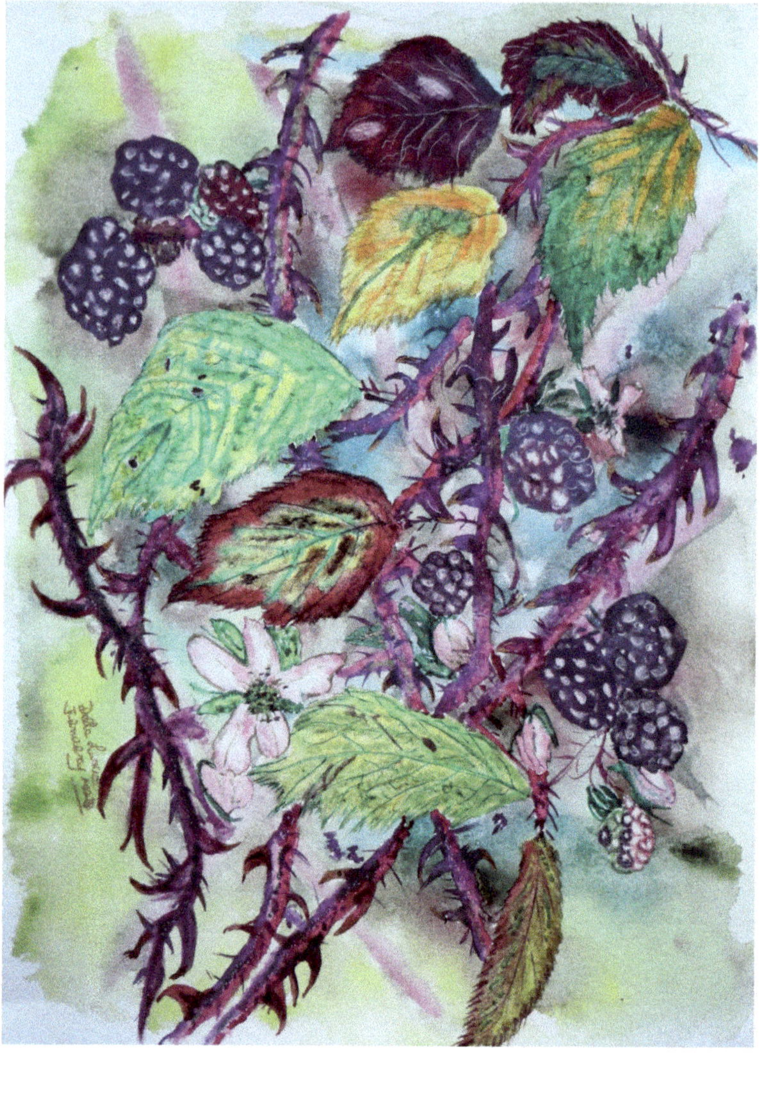

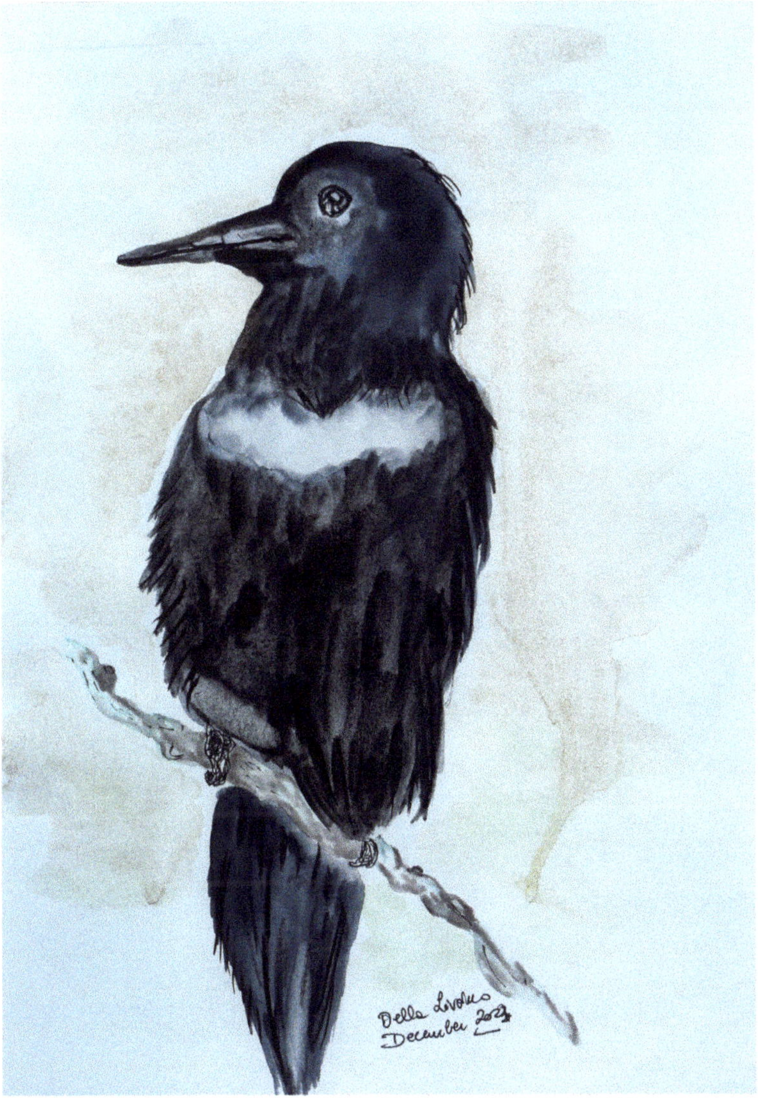

214

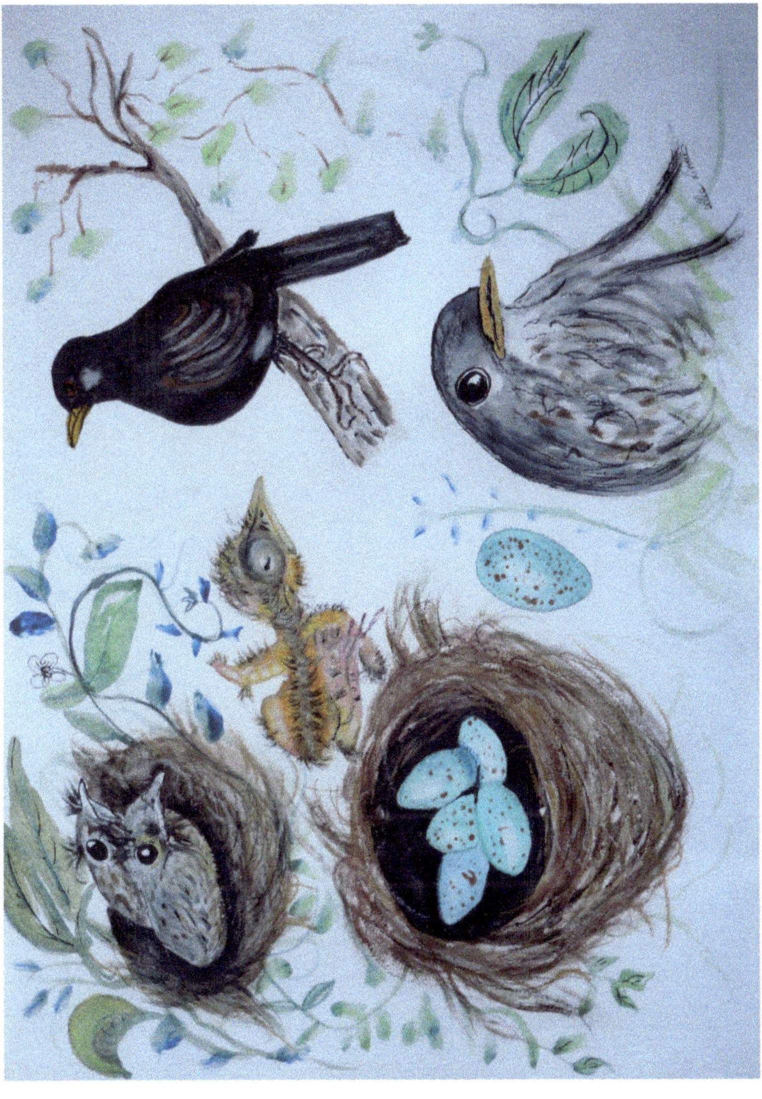

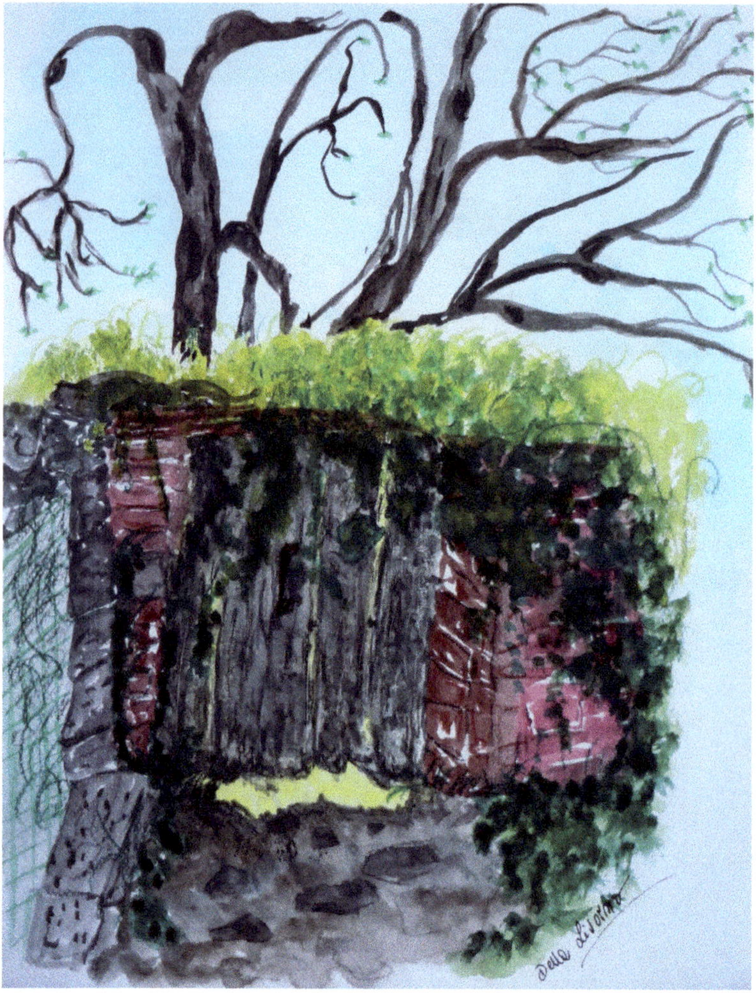

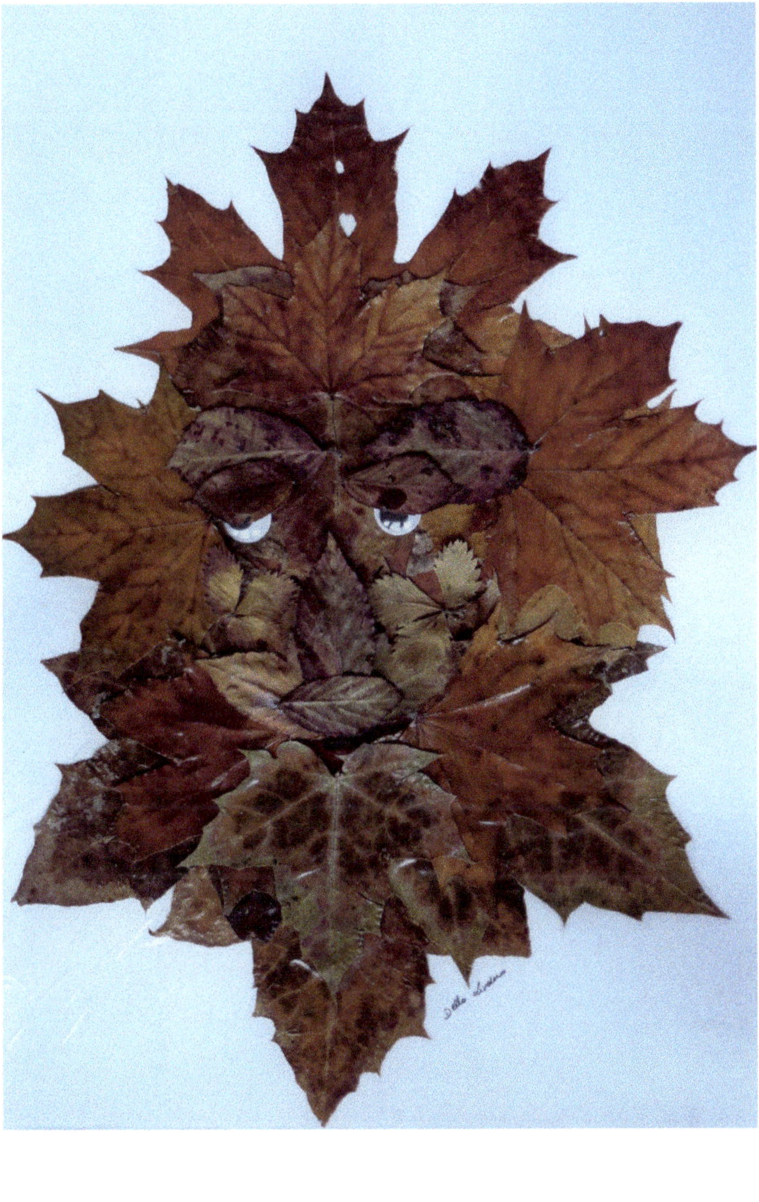

Acknowledgements

I wish to thank my husband, Alan, for his support including copyediting, formatting and submitting this work for publishing.

BOOKS BY THE SAME AUTHOR

- Come una foglia d'autunno.
- Una vita migliore.
- Miagliano reawakens to the magic touch and scent of wool.
- The adventures of Nigel Sheep. A small sheep with big ambitions. / Le avventure di Pecora Nigel. Una piccola pecora con grandi ambizioni.
- Miagliano e i suoi segreti: guida illustrata al villaggio post-industriale di Miagliano.
- The weird case of Auntie Doris

All books are available on Lulu.com and Amazon.com

Milton Keynes UK
Ingram Content Group UK Ltd.
UKHW021224170324
439505UK00007BA/13